HERBS

THEIR CULTIVATION AND USAGE

HERBS

THEIR
CULTIVATION
AND
USAGE

John and Rosemary
HEMPHILL

BLANDFORD

CONTENTS

Introduction   7

Hints on using fresh
and dried herbs   8

Points to remember when
propagating and cultivating herbs   10

The herb garden   15
The herbs   17
Angelica   18
Anise   20
Balm   22
Basil   24
Bay Tree   26
Bergamot   29
Borage   31
Caraway   33
Chamomile   35
Chervil   38
Chicory   40
Chives   42
Comfrey   44
Coriander   46
Cress   48

Dill	50
Fennel, Florence	52
Garlic	54
Horseradish	56
Lavender	58
Lovage	62
Marjoram and Oregano	64
Mint	67
Parsley	73
Rosemary	76
Sage	79
Salad Burnet	81
Savory	83
Sorrel, French	85
Tarragon, French	87
Thyme	90
Recipes	96
Herb Chart	120
Herb Tea Chart	123
Reference Books	124
Index	125

ACKNOWLEDGEMENTS

Our warm thanks to Ann Ferns, Reg Morrison, Anne Wilson, Warwick Jacobson and Mark Newman of Lansdowne Press for their caring interest and guidance in producing this book.

Grateful thanks also to Clare Wilmot of The Triad Clinic for allowing us to call on her wide knowledge of herbal medicine in some of our research for the medicinal sections of the book.

DEDICATION:

For Gretta Anna and David Teplitzky

INTRODUCTION

There is a tremendous number of different kinds of herbs. Broadly, they may be grouped into three main categories, which are, culinary, scented and medicinal. Many of them have a variety of other uses, but for this book we have concentrated on culinary herbs which most people are able to grow and would like to have for everyday use in the kitchen, or for making perfumed gifts. Their medicinal use is touched on for interesting historical knowledge and a few simple remedies are given, as are their cosmetic uses and value in companion planting and insect repellent properties.

When planning to grow herbs, choose a place near the kitchen for convenience. They can be grown in a rockery, along a small pathway leading to a sundial or birdbath, or in their own formal garden, with set patterns dividing the beds.

There are many different kinds of containers to use for growing herbs in flats or units. First it must be remembered that herbs are not indoor plants and will not give their true fragrance without fresh air and some sunshine during the day. If there is not a balcony or porch, it is still possible to grow the smaller herbs in troughs or pots on a window sill, or in hanging baskets in an open window. Where there is room, a terra cotta "strawberry jar" with several apertures around the sides as well as the top, making spaces for approximately five different herbs, is an excellent idea. There are also super-large pots with apertures for twelve or more herbs.

Select plants with small root systems for these pots. There is a choice of parsley, chives, chervil, land cress, sage, various kinds of culinary thymes, marjoram, oregano, savory and salad burnet. In the top you can grow a rosemary bush, a small bay tree (to be re-potted as they grow) and bush basil during the summer. There are also troughs on the market made in terra-cotta, stone, plastic, polythene and natural hollowed out tree-trunks or branches, as well as a variety of hanging baskets in a selection of sizes. The containers must be filled with a fairly rich, light soil mixture, so that the plants will have nourishment as they grow, and yet will be able to drain properly. Never let herbs in pots dry out. They also should be fed occasionally. We find one of the brands of slow-release "plant pills" which are available, is excellent for this. Instructions on how often to use it is given on the package.

John Hemphill   Rosemary Hemphill

HINTS ON USING
FRESH AND DRIED
HERBS

When giving information in the culinary, medicinal and cosmetic sections in this book the measurements for using fresh herbs are given. However, there are many people who are unable to grow their own, and as fresh herbs are not always available anyway, a general rule to follow is to use *half* the amount of the dried product. Of course this will also depend on the potency of the dried herbs, so test for flavour on the tip of the tongue. Correctly dried herbs always taste stronger than the fresh, as only the watery content has evaporated, leaving a concentration of essential oils. Whole dried leaves, or chopped or crumbled dried leaves are more powerful in fragrance and taste than powdered herbs, which often include ground stalks as well.

Information on harvesting, drying and freezing is given for each herb in its separate section, as their requirements vary. If growing your own herbs, it is best to gather them as needed for highest nutritive value. If you wish to keep them fresh for a few days, take newly picked, washed sprays, shake off the excess water, wrap in foil or plastic, and store in the refrigerator. Freshly chopped herbs may be kept for about a week in the same way.

For freezing herbs, the most practical way — and the quickest — is to pick fresh sprays, wash them well, remove stalks, then chop finely. Put the chopped herbs into ice-cube trays, with just a little water, and freeze. Alternatively put herb sprigs (without stalks) into a blender or food chopper with a little water, then chop finely. Freeze in ice-cube trays as before, and remove the blocks as required: they can be dropped straight into hot cooking, and will melt in a few minutes. Use a little less of the frozen herbs than the fresh, as freezing tends to give them a slightly bitter flavour. Most herbs are suitable for this type of treatment even basil, whose leaves bruise and discolour very easily in our experience, although there are no such problems when drying the foliage.

One of the pleasures of cultivating a herb garden is the availability of a variety of herbs for use in the kitchen all the year round.

POINTS TO REMEMBER WHEN
PROPAGATING
AND
CULTIVATING HERBS

Cuttings

When taking cuttings from a parent plant, always keep them in water, or wrapped in a damp cloth until ready to put in the sand. Do not let them wilt.

Use coarse river sand for striking cuttings, never use beach sand as it is too fine and probably contains salt.

When preparing cuttings, always pull off leaves with an upward pull, or use secateurs to avoid tearing the bark of the plant.

When removing leaves from cuttings, one-third of the foliage should be left on top.

Never push a cutting into the sand; always make a hole first with a knitting needle or skewer slightly thicker than the cutting.

Trim cuttings with a sharp knife or secateurs just below a leaf node. Moisten the ends of the cuttings, then dip lower 1 cm (½ inch) into a suitable cutting powder. Shake off excess powder and insert cuttings one-third of the way into the sand. Try to cover at least two leaf nodes, and more if possible.

When cuttings are first put in sand, flood with water so the sand will

The correct way to take a cutting is just below a leaf node, snipping with a sharp knife or secateurs.

pack tightly around the cuttings, then keep sand moist at all times.

Rooted cuttings can be taken from the sand and planted directly into the

A rosemary cutting which has made good roots and is ready to be put into a small pot of potting mixture.

Cuttings should be placed in coarse river sand to strike. First make a hole slightly thicker than the cutting with a sharp object such as a knitting needle.

When inserting cuttings into the sand, they should be packed closely together and the sand kept moist.

For the best results, rooted cuttings should be put in small, separate pots in semi-shade for a few weeks.

ground, but to obtain best results with a minimum amount of loss, grow them in small separate pots in semi-shade for several weeks first.

Cuttings must be watered daily.

To help cuttings make roots in cool climates, place them in a glass house, or if this is not possible, lay a sheet of glass over a box, making sure the glass is painted with white-wash to prevent the plants being scorched by the sun's rays.

Seeds

When sowing seeds always keep the seed bed, or box, moist at all times, as drying out even for a short period can cause germination to cease.

Put seed box on a level surface, as accidental over watering or heavy rain can wash the covering soil and seed to one end of the box.

Pots or tubs must be filled to about 1.2 cm (½ inch) from the top to allow for easy watering.

When covering seed in a box, the soil should be rubbed through the hands so that it is fine and powdry and any hard lumps should be discarded.

When preparing a seed box, furrows for the planting of the seeds can be made with a piece of timber.

Seed boxes should be placed on a level surface and the seeds sown along the furrows.

The soil on top of freshly sown seeds should be firmly pressed down.

12

Cultivating Herbs

A well drained porous or sandy soil is preferred by nearly all herbs, unless stated otherwise in their sections. They do not like soil enriched with fertilisers and manures, although garden compost is always helpful. If the ground is heavy, dig it well first, and if sour add some lime before planting. Rockeries are excellent places for growing herbs.

A sunny, open situation suits most herbs best. Where this is not so it has been stated.

Cut old growth and dead wood away regularly to give new growth a chance and to improve the appearance of the plant.

A tray of healthy young sage seedlings which have reached a stage where they can be potted up.

Herbs in our experience have remained free from diseases. However, many of them are vulnerable to leaf-eating pests such as slugs, snails, caterpillars and small beetles. Snail bait will look after the slugs and snails, and a routine twice-weekly dusting with Derris Dust (a non-poisonous old remedy) on dampened foliage should take care of the caterpillars and beetles. For those who wish to build up the strength of their gardens so as to try and eradicate all pests, we recommend a comprehensive book on this subject, *Companion Plants* by Helen Philbrick and Richard B. Gregg, published by Stuart and Watkins, London. This book deals with the placing of certain plants near one another or not, according to their make-up, for compatibility, and as insect repellents.

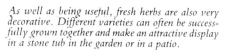

As well as being useful, fresh herbs are also very decorative. Different varieties can often be successfully grown together and make an attractive display in a stone tub in the garden or in a patio.

This clump of pennyroyal is being prepared for propagation by root division. The herbs are divided up into sections using sharp secateurs.

This rosemary is a well-established plant which was potted as a cutting and has grown to a stage where it can be transferred to a garden bed.

When clumps of herb seedlings are separated for propagation by the root division method, it is very important to ensure that each section has an adequate piece of established root attached.

During the weeks that it has been in the pot, the rosemary cutting has developed a good root system. In cool climates, roots can be encouraged by placing cuttings in a glasshouse or under glass sheets.

THE HERB GARDEN

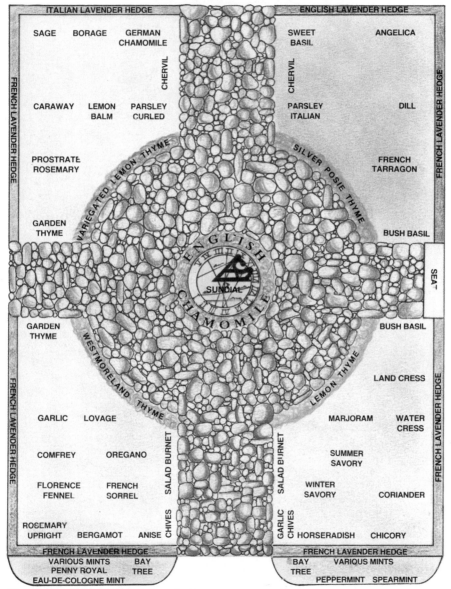

| ITALIAN LAVENDER HEDGE | ENGLISH LAVENDER HEDGE |

FRENCH LAVENDER HEDGE

SAGE   BORAGE   GERMAN CHAMOMILE

SWEET BASIL   ANGELICA

CHERVIL

CHERVIL

CARAWAY   LEMON BALM   PARSLEY CURLED

PARSLEY ITALIAN   DILL

PROSTRATE ROSEMARY

VARIEGATED LEMON THYME

SILVER POSIE THYME

FRENCH TARRAGON

GARDEN THYME

BUSH BASIL

ENGLISH CHAMOMILE

SUNDIAL

SEA

GARDEN THYME

WESTMORELAND THYME

BUSH BASIL

LEMON THYME

LAND CRESS

GARLIC   LOVAGE

MARJORAM   WATER CRESS

COMFREY   OREGANO

SALAD BURNET

SALAD BURNET

SUMMER SAVORY

FLORENCE FENNEL   FRENCH SORREL

WINTER SAVORY   CORIANDER

ROSEMARY UPRIGHT   BERGAMOT   ANISE

CHIVES

GARLIC CHIVES

HORSERADISH   CHICORY

| FRENCH LAVENDER HEDGE | FRENCH LAVENDER HEDGE |

VARIOUS MINTS   BAY
PENNY ROYAL   TREE
EAU-DE-COLOGNE MINT

BAY
TREE   VARIOUS MINTS
PEPPERMINT   SPEARMINT

The best aspect for a herb garden is facing the direction in which it will get sun for most of the day, so that plants will gain the maximum benefit from the sun's rays. The soil should be light for good drainage.

THE
HERBS

ANGELICA

(Angelica archangelica) Umbelliferae.
Biennial.

Propagation: *seeds. Spring (Autumn in temperate climates) within a week of collecting.*
Position: *shady, sheltered.*
Soil: *rich.*
Height: *1.50m-2.40m (5-8 feet).*
Part used: *seeds, leaves, stalks, roots.*

Description

Angelica has serrated, bright green leaves and branching, hollow stems with a celery-like texture. The round, whitish-green flower-heads bloom in late spring in the second year of growth. When not allowed to flower at all by frequent cutting of the stems, the plant will continue to flourish for several seasons instead of for the customary two years. Angelica is completely permeated by a unique essence, giving it a delicately sweet and refreshing aroma.

History and mythology

The history of angelica goes far back into the legends and folklore of Northern Europe, and in particular the countries of Lapland, Iceland and Russia. Because of its wonderfully benign qualities, both in the physical and spiritual realms, the plant held an important place in pagan rites, and later in Christian festivals. According to legend, during the Middle Ages, an angel appeared to a monk in a dream and revealed that angelica would cure the plague. This is why the herb was called *angelica*, the guardian angel.

Cultivation

When sowing angelica, it is very important to use only fresh seed, as the germinating period is very short. The seed can be sown in pre-pared boxes, or in the open ground. When seedlings are about 8 cm (3 inches) high, plant them out 90 cm (3 feet) apart in a moist and shady position. Rich soil and some shelter are essential for maximum growth. In poor ground, plants will become stunted and the leaves yellow.

Harvesting and processing

Harvest the seed just before it starts to fall, by snipping off and drying whole flower-heads. Sift out any dried husks and stalks, and store the seed in airtight containers for household use. But if required for sowing, plant the seed out within a week at the most. The stems can be cut and used at any time; however, their full flavour and size are best just after flowering. The root is stored by digging, washing and keeping it in an airy, dry place until needed. The leaves may be cut from the stems and laid on sheets of clean paper or racks, in a shady, warm place until dry. When brittle, crumble them into airtight containers.

Various Uses

Culinary

A few young angelica leaves may be added to salads. The hollow stems and stalks can be crystallized and used for decorating sweets and cakes, and if you do not candy your own stems, they can be bought in many shops. The stems and stalks, either candied or fresh, give

their sweet flavour and goodness to stewed fruits, especially acid fruit like rhubarb and plums, and to jams and jellies. The roots can be cooked and eaten like a vegetable.

Medicinal

Angelica was valued as a protection against all sorts of infections. It was used as an aid to digestion. One old remedy for flatulence directed that the stalks be slowly chewed until the condition was relieved, which was good advice, as it has been found that one of angelica's constituents is pectin, an enzyme which acts on the digesting of food. Another of the plant's components is a resin stimulating to the lungs and to the skin. In the cold countries where it was known best, angelica was prized for its ability to give a sensation of warmth when it was eaten or taken as a tea. (A tea can be made from either the leaves, stems, seeds or the dried root.) Modern-day herbalists still recommend angelica tea to calm the nerves, to relieve colds and influenza and as a long-term preventive against winter illnesses. Many available herb tea blends contain angelica for its therapeutic properties and for its pleasant flavour. A number of the old herbalists regarded angelica as the most powerful of all medicinal plants, every part of it — roots,

Delicately perfumed angelica enjoys a shaded spot in the garden and thrives in a rich soil. The flowers appear in the spring of the second year of growth.

stems, leaves and seeds — having health-giving properties. People with a tendency to diabetes are warned against it however, as it may increase sugar in the urine. The subtle aroma which suffuses the whole herb makes it an important ingredient in many luxury beverages, including vermouth and some liqueurs, such as Chartreuse. The earliest liqueurs were prepared in mediaeval monasteries, orginally as medicines.

Cosmetic

Angelica seeds are used in the making of some perfumes. Dried angelica leaves go into a pot-pourri mixture and are an ingredient in sweet-smelling herb pillows. Use fresh or dried leaves (in a muslin bag) in a hot bath for relaxation and fragrance.

Companion planting

It has been noted that the common stinging nettle *(Urtica dioica)*, when grown near certain plants, intensifies their essential oil content. In the case of angelica, this is increased by as much as 80 percent.

19

ANISE

(Pimpinella anisum) Umbelliferae.
  Annual

Propagation: *seed. Spring (and again*
  in Autumn in temperate climates).
Position: *sheltered, sunny.*
Soil: *light, well drained.*
Height: *45 cm-60 cm (1½-2 feet).*
Part used: *seeds, foliage sometimes.*

Description

Anise has feathery leaves and flat, white flower-heads which bloom in late summer. Aromatic, small, brown seeds or fruit follow, with a strong licorice taste, most of them having a distinguishing fine hair at one end. The seed is the most useful part of the plant.

History and mythology

Anise is native to the Middle East and was known in ancient Egypt. Its usefulness as a fragrant and health-giving herb spread to Greece and Rome and then to many other countries. The Romans discovered that the seeds of anise and other aromatic spices helped the digestion after large banquets, so these spices were incorporated into a special cake which was served at the end of a large meal, such as a marriage feast. This is said to be the origin of today's spicy wedding cake. Aniseed was grown by the monks in monastery gardens during the Middle Ages, for use as a tea.

Cultivation

Because of its spindly nature, this herb needs protection from prevailing winds and, at the same time, plenty of sunshine to promote healthy growth. The seedlings are soft and fragile and do not transplant well, so it is best to sow directly into the ground. Make sure that the soil is well broken up and in fine seed bed condition, adding a little lime if the ground is very acid. Unless the soil is extremely poor, fertilizer is not necessary. Sow the seeds in spring, and again in autumn in temperate zones, in 12 mm (½ inch) deep drills, 30 cm (12 inches) apart. Cover and pack the soil down well, then keep moist until the seedlings appear. Water regularly in hot, dry weather, preferably in the late afternoon or evening, so as not to scorch the plants.

Harvesting and processing

Harvesting the fruit when it is ripe is simple. After the flower-umbels have become heavy with full, brown seeds, cut the heads off before they drop. Store them in cardboard boxes, or on sheets of paper, in a dry place, exposing them to direct sunlight when possible, to completely dry out any moisture.

Sun-drying is not good for herb leaves, but is helpful in the drying of seed-heads. When they are crisp and dry, rub the seeds between the palms of the hands. The husks and old flower-heads are easily removed by sifting the seeds through a sieve. Store them in labelled and dated airtight containers. For culinary, medicinal or cosmetic use, the seed will last for many years. But for propagating, germination will be more successful if the seeds are sown the following season.

The early leaves on anise cuttings are rounded, while those that develop later are more frondy.

Various uses

Culinary

Warmly licorice-tasting aniseed, whether whole or ground, flavours and helps to digest many different types of food, such as breads, pasta, cakes and biscuits, as well as stewed or baked apples and pears. For the same reason, it is used with some vegetables which can be indigestible, such as cabbages, onions, cucumbers, carrots, turnips and beetroot. It is used, too, in some rich cheese dishes. The leaves of anise are sometimes used in food — they give a piquant touch to salads. They may also be added to broths and soups while cooking.

Medicinal

Aniseed not only works on the digestive system, but also helps respiratory ailments. The plant's volatile oil contains anethole, the substance which has such a beneficial effect on the digestion. Aniseed tea, taken regularly, is said to allay colds and influenza, relieve flatulence, brighten the eyes and make the breath sweeter. Anise is used to flavour cough lozenges, some cordials, herb tea blends, and liqueurs, such as Anisette. A little powdered seed added to food for young children will help their digestion, and when some aniseed tea is mixed with warm milk and honey, it helps soothe a fretful child. It is wise to give these simple home remedies in moderation to the very young. This applies to all medicinal herbs, unless prescribed by a fully-trained therapist. The full flavour of aniseed tea is brought out by crushing the seeds before putting them into the teapot. Allow them to draw a little longer than usual.

Cosmetic

The Romans used aniseed in perfumes, as did the Britons in the Middle Ages. Cooled aniseed tea gently sponged onto the face with cotton wool helps to lighten the skin. Anise oil is also a good, fragrant antiseptic and has been used as an ingredient in dentifrices.

Companion planting

The seed of anise will germinate quicker and grow better if it is sown near coriander seed. It has been observed that the presence of coriander improves the actual seed formation of the anise plants.
N.B. there is another anise called star anise which comes from a tree, *Illicium anisatum*, that is indigenous to China. The oil from these seeds is the same in composition as the annual anise, and equally effective medicinally.

BALM

(Melissa officinalis) Labiatae.
Perennial.

Propagation: *seeds, cuttings, root*
division. Spring (Autumn in temperate
zones).
Position: *part sun.*
Soil: *moist, rich.*
Height: *75 cm (2½ feet).*
Part used: *leaves.*

Description

The strongly lemon-scented foliage of this
herb gives it the popular name of "lemon
balm". The leaves are crinkly and shaped like
mint leaves, although larger in size. The small,
white flowers, which bloom in summer, grow
in clusters along a thin, angular stem. The
plant has a spreading habit, and the shallow
roots are thick and matted.

History and mythology

Balm is native to the mountainous regions of
Southern Europe and was used as one of the
sacred herbs in the temple of Diana. Its botanical name of *Melissa* is Latin for "bee", as
these insects are constant visitors to the nectar-
laden blossoms when they are in flower. (How
intricate is the world of nature, for when wax
is poured into the honeyed flowers of the *Labi-*
atae family, which includes amongst its mem-
bers thyme, sage, oregano, marjoram, mint
and rosemary as well as balm, the hardened
shape that results is identical with the bee's
proboscis, the organ it uses for extracting
honey). The name of balm has been abbre-
viated from the fragrant oil balsam, signifying
the herb's aromatic sweetness. Bee-hives were
traditionally rubbed with sweet-smelling
herbs, especially balm leaves, to help keep the
hive together and to attract homing bees.
Honey was regarded as a necessary commo-
dity for the household larders of bygone days,
and there was much written about the art of
bee-keeping, those who lived close to these
industrious insects having a great respect for
their wisdom. Herb gardens and bee-hives
were traditionally linked together, and
Thomas Hyll writes in 1579 that the hives

should be placed near: "...the hearbe
Baulme... ; and manye other sweete and
wholesome floures."

Cultivation

The simplest way to propagate balm is by root
division in spring, just as the new growth is
starting. If you prefer to propagate by taking
cuttings, wait for the new tips to grow to
about 8 cm (3 inches) long, and when firm
enough, take a 10 cm (4 inch) long tip,
removing all the leaves except the top two.
Press the cuttings deeply into a pot of river
sand, leaving one third of each cutting exposed. Sow the seed in spring, (or in autumn
in temperate climates), into a prepared box, or
in shallow drills straight into the ground,
leaving a little space between plants. If seeds
are sown fairly thickly, or seedlings are planted close together over an area of several feet, a
large clump will develop quickly. In certain
areas the leaves of balm seedlings can get frost-
bitten: under these conditions, plant in a
sheltered position where there will be some
sun during the day. If the seedlings are grown
in too wet and shady a place, fungus may give
some trouble. Lastly, watch carefully for leaf-
eating grubs and insects. If they occur,

The piquant lemon fragrance of balm makes it an interesting seasoning for chicken, fish, lamb or pork. In the garden, balm foliage grows densely and has a spreading habit with shallow roots.

sprinkle the dampened foliage with one of the more natural insect repellent powders on the market.

Harvesting and processing

When drying balm for storing purposes, cut the stalks back almost to ground level just as the flowers begin to appear, and dry them on airy racks in a shady place. They may also be tied loosely together in bunches and hung to dry. Immediately the leaves are crisp and dry, rub them from their stalks and keep them in airtight containers. Fresh balm may be picked in sprays, washed, wrapped in foil and put in the refrigerator where it will stay fresh for a week or two. For longer lasting results, fresh leaves may be chopped finely, put into ice cube trays with a little water and frozen until needed.

Various uses

Culinary

Fresh or dried balm leaves go well in fruit or vegetable salads, milk puddings and in certain soups. The fresh lemon fragrance of the herb enhances buttered, cooked vegetables. For a change, balm makes an excellent seasoning for chicken, fish, lamb or pork. It is traditional to add fresh sprigs of balm to wine cups and fruit drinks. Chopped balm leaves may be added to stewed fruit. They are also delicious as a filling for sandwiches. Balm tea is particularly refreshing and reviving in the summer, even one leaf in the teapot with Indian tea will give a

lift to both palate and spirits.

Medicinal

Balm leaves contain essences which were highly valued for their healing properties, and were used in treating many ailments such as melancholy, nervous headache, failing memory, neuralgia and fevers. Balm tea is still taken today to help bring down high temperatures and to lessen the effects of exhaustion in hot weather. Together with sage, balm was said to contribute to longevity. It was also used to guard against senility. Balm has been widely used continuously for many years because of its tonic effect on the stomach. It assists in the digestion of food and is said to increase the appetite.

Cosmetic

Balm tea is used for outward as well as inward purposes. It cleanses and perfumes the skin, and for this reason, is used with other herbs in the bath water. An infusion for the bath should be made several times stronger than when balm is taken as a beverage. It is used as an infusion with verbena and other ingredients to make a natural cleansing cream. An infusion as a mouth wash sweetens the breath. The dried whole leaves of lemon balm make an excellent addition to a pot-pourri mixture and to a soothing blend for a sleep pillow.

Companion planting

It has been noted that balm plants in borders, together with certain other herbs, are helpful to all vegetables. Lemon balm in pastures is believed to increase the milk production in cows, and is also strengthening and soothing when given to them, together with marjoram, as a tea after calving.

BASIL

Basil, Sweet: *(Ocimum basilicum)*
    Labiatae. Annual.
Basil, Bush: *(O. minimum) Labiatae.*
    Annual

Propagation: *seeds. Late Spring, early*
    Summer.
Position: *sunny, sheltered.*
Soil: *light to sandy, well drained.*
Height: *sweet basil, 75 cm (2½ feet).*
    bush basil, 30 cm (12 inches).
Part used: *leaves.*

Description

There are different types of basil plants with
varying scents, flavours and leaf colouration.
Just a few are mentioned here. One kind has
foliage with a distinct aroma of camphor,
which is interesting, but does not encourage
one to eat it. Another type we have grown has
reddish stalks and coarse, shiny, green leaves
which have a typical basil aroma and could be
used for flavouring soups. But the leaves are
too tough to be palatable when eaten raw.
There is also an ornamental, colourful variety
of sweet basil, with rich, purple leaves and
pale pink flowers. It is an attractive garden
plant and is highly perfumed. However, the
actual flavour is rank and is not recommended
for cooking purposes. The old favourites,
sweet basil and bush basil are still the best
varieties to grow for the kitchen. The tender
foliage of both these basils is bright green,
with a spicy, clove-like aroma. Sweet basil
leaves have a stronger perfume than the leaves
of bush basil, which are also much smaller.
Both varieties have small, white, lipped
flowers in the autumn.

History and mythology

Basil originated in India, where it was regarded as a sacred herb. It was also known in
ancient Egypt, Greece and Rome and there are
many different legends concerning it. The
unique and pronounced fragrance it releases
into the surrounding atmosphere must have
caused much speculation as to the plant's
attributes among the wise ancients, who were
close to the elemental world. Basil's botanical
name of *basilicum* has kingly associations. One
early writer said that the smell was so excellent, that it was "fit for a king's house". On
the other hand, some say that the name was
derived from *basilisk*, a mythical serpent-like
creature that could kill with a look, and for
many years the plant was linked with poison
and "venomous beasts". At the same time an
application of the herb was prescribed to draw
out the poison from stings and bites.

Cultivation

As basil must have warm conditions, early
spring sowing is not advised. For best results,
sow the seed at the end of spring, or at the
beginning of summer. Both basils are susceptible to cold weather and are very frost-
tender too. A cold change will kill the plants,
even though there may be no frost. Sow the
seed directly into the ground in shallow drills.
If the soil is sour, lime it well two weeks before
planting, making sure that the bed is well
broken up and as fine as possible. If the soil is
heavy, a small quantity of river sand will help
to make the ground more suitable, both for
sowing and drainage. When sweet basil is 8 cm

Bush basil, like sweet basil, is a very versatile herb, often grown for its many uses in the kitchen.

Sweet basil is a popular culinary herb and is included in a number of dishes, including pasta.

(3 inches) high, thin out to 30 cm (12 inches) between plants. For bush basil, a distance of 15 cm (6 inches) between seedlings is sufficient. As the plants grow, it is important to pinch out the centres to ensure a spreading, bushy habit. Bush basil is a very suitable plant for growing in pots, as it is so compact. An 18 cm (7 inch) pot is an excellent size for this. Fill the container with potting soil, and sow three to four seeds in it. Water them well and keep them moist to ensure germination and satisfactory growth. When the seedlings are 8 cm (3 inches) high, choose the sturdiest looking one to leave in the pot, then prick out the rest, which may be planted into other containers or into the open ground. Remember that basil (or any other herb) will not grow as an indoor plant; a sunny terrace, or a window sill where there is sunshine and fresh air, is the ideal position.

Harvesting and processing

It is necessary to harvest basil in the early autumn before the cold weather turns the leaves limp and yellow. (In hot climates, basil grows throughout the year, and under these conditions, the seeds will often self-sow). For fullest flavour, cut long, leafy stalks for drying just before the plant comes into flower, spreading them out in a shady place or wire mesh to encourage quick drying. Do not hang them in bunches, as the soft foliage will then dry too slowly and may possibly spoil. Oven drying is not satisfactory, as the leaves, which bruise easily, are liable to scorch. Fresh basil leaves may be chopped finely, mixed with a little water and frozen in ice cube trays to be used when needed. Basil, together with pine nuts, garlic, oil, and Parmesan cheese may be made into *pestou* (a Mediterranean sauce) and frozen. Basil butter (chopped basil leaves pounded into butter then cut into squares when cold) may also be satisfactorily frozen in sealed polythene bags.

Various uses

Culinary

Basil's mouth-watering aroma makes it a versatile herb to use in many different types of food. It has a special affinity with tomatoes, and tomato-based dishes and is excellent with eggplant, zucchini, marrow, squash and spinach. Added during the last half hour of cooking, it gives zest to pea soup and lentil soup. It is delicious with cream cheese in sandwiches, gives a lift to green salads and sliced cucumbers and is excellent in all pasta dishes. As mentioned above, it is the main ingredient

in *pestou*, for which there are varying recipes (one of which is given on page 99), but all contain basil, which is essential to its character. Basil also goes well with poultry, veal, liver, kidneys, fish and shellfish and makes a savoury vinegar when the leaves are steeped in it for a few weeks.

In this traditional-style garden, sweet basil makes an attractive border around flagstones and a sundial.

Medicinal

Basil's old connection with poison has been interpreted by one modern herbalist as an antidote to much that is not wholesome in today's food. Basil has long been a herbal remedy for diseases of the brain, heart, lungs and kidneys and bladder. It is often mixed with borage to make a healthful, palatable, tonic tea to revive lowered vitality. The dried leaves have been made into snuff as a remedy for headaches and colds.

The leaves of bush basil are smaller than those of sweet basil and its fragrance is less strong.

Cosmetic

Basil leaves have been preserved by an old method which directs that alternate layers of fresh leaves, coarse sea salt and vegetable oil be put in a preserving jar and sealed. Later the aromatic mixture is strained and the resulting fragrant oil used as a toning body rub. An infusion of basil in wine is sometimes used on the skin to close enlarged pores.

Companion planting

Basil plants help to enliven and stimulate vegetables growing in the garden, especially tomatoes. After close observation by an eminent gardener of our acquaintance, it was noted that basil also helped to repel white fly, which is troublesome to tomatoes. It is said that basil and rue do not grow well near each other.

BAY TREE

(Laurus nobilis) Lauraceae. Perennial.

Propagation: *seeds, cuttings. Spring.*
Position: *sunny, open.*
Soil: *good quality.*
Height: *11m (40 feet).*
Part used: *leaves.*

Bay leaves

Description

The bay is a very large, attractive tree, thickly covered with glossy, dark green leaves, which are narrow and approximately 10 cm (4 inches) long. When broken, they give off a warmly pungent aroma. Bay trees make excellent tub specimens, especially if grown as standards, when the lower branching stems are cut off and the tops are pruned into rounded shapes. In Europe and America they are often grown like this, either in gardens or on each side of a doorway, particularly in front of hotels and clubs. They look very elegant when treated in this way. The bay tree is native to the shores of the Mediterranean and among its popular names are "sweet bay", "bay laurel", "Roman laurel", "noble laurel", and "true laurel". There is another type of laurel, the cherry laurel *(Prunus laurocerasus)*, which is poisonous and must not be confused with the bay tree. In spring, the tight, white flower-buds burst into waxy, cream blossoms with pronounced yellow stamens. When in flower, the tree is continually visited by swarms of bees. The flowers are followed by purple berries that go black and hard when dried.

History and mythology

When looking at this tree growing in our gardens, or when using the leaves in cooking, it is interesting to think about the old traditions and history associated with the bay. In early Greece and Rome, the greatest honour for those who were victorious on the battle-field, and in the sports arena, was to be crowned with a bay laurel wreath — as were outstanding men of letters too, hence the title of "poet laureate". The bay laurel was a part of pagan temple rites and ceremonies.

Cultivation

To propagate bay trees, cuttings are advised, as the seeds do not germinate readily. The seeds are about the size of a pea and are very hard, like a nut. It is necessary to sow them at least 25 mm (1 inch) below the soil's surface. Do not be disappointed if there is only about 5 percent germination. Cuttings are taken when the new spring leaves have hardened. Each cutting should be 15 cm (6 inches) long, and of new wood. Break the cutting away from the old wood, leaving a heel 6 mm (¼ inch) long, which must be trimmed carefully with a sharp knife to eliminate any bark which overhangs the heel. Strip the bottom leaves off the cutting, leaving two-thirds of bare stalk to press into a pot of wet river sand, firming it in with the fingers. Keep cuttings watered at all times. By the end of spring they should have made roots and will be ready to plant out into containers holding potting mixture. It is always advisable to establish slow-growing plants such as bay trees in pots for at least a year, rather than put them straight into the garden. Bay trees are susceptible to white wax scale, which makes the foliage sooty and unattractive, and also causes poor leaf growth. This can be controlled by spraying with white oil in hot weather, or scrubbing the affected places with soapy water.

Harvesting and processing

The leaves can be used for cooking at any time during the year. If you wish to dry them, the best way is pick the leaves off the stalks, then spread them out on a wire rack, where they will dry quickly with a good, green colour. An alternative is to hang leafy branches in bunches in a dark, airy place.

Various uses

Culinary

Bay leaves are indispensable in many different types of cooking. For instance, a bay leaf is an essential ingredient in a "bouquet garni", or savoury herb posy, the other herbs being a spray each of parsley, marjoram and thyme and a few peppercorns. These are tied together and dropped into casseroles, soups, or stews, and removed after cooking. Or, the dried herbs, including the bay, may be crushed and crumbled together to make a blend, which is then put straight into the pot and left to amalgamate into the stock during cooking. As a variation, when cooking an Italian-type casserole or soup, add oregano and a little garlic and leave out the marjoram and thyme. For fish, replace the marjoram and thyme with dill. For lamb, replace the marjoram and thyme with rosemary. Bay leaves on their own flavour soups and casseroles; boiled, baked or steamed fish; meat and poultry. A bay leaf gives a pungent aroma to marinades, and if a leaf is placed on top of a milk pudding as it goes into the oven, a subtle and unusual flavour is imparted.

The bay tree, with its pleasing shape and dark, shiny leaves is often grown for ornamental purposes.

Medicinal

There has been found in the bark of stem and root, volatile oil, starch, several acids, resins and a red colouring substance. The bay had an important place in early medicine. Externally, an oil from the leaves and berries was applied to bruises and sprains. The oil was also dropped into the ears to relieve pain and was used to treat rheumatism, hysteria and flatulence. The powdered berries were sometimes prescribed to improve the appetite and cure fevers.

Cosmetic

A facial steam bath containing herbs to clear the skin was popular with our grandmothers and has become so again today. For normal skins, a mixture of bay leaves, chamomile flowers, rosemary and rose petals is recommended. Dried bay leaves go into pot-pourri

An avenue of bay trees gives a gracious air of Mediterranean elegance to a garden.

blends, and with other soothing herbs, into sleep pillows for insomnia.

Companion planting

We have found that other plants will grow happily near pungent bay trees, except when the tree becomes too large and the root system robs the nearby soil of nourishment.

BERGAMOT

(Monarda didyma) Labiatae. Perennial.

Propagation: *seeds, root division.*
　Spring.
Position: *shady, morning sun.*
Soil: *rich, moist.*
Height: *1.20m (4 feet).*
Part used: *leaves, flowers.*

Description

The flowers of bergamot, in size, colour and form, are amongst the showiest of all herb blossoms. There are several different colours, varying in hue from pink and mauve to a rich red, which is the popular Cambridge Scarlet. Bergamot's slightly hairy leaves are oval — approximately 8 cm (3 inches) long and are attached in pairs to square stems. The pom-pom type flowers start blooming on 90 cm (3 feet) tall stalks in early summer. If the plants are in the right position, where the roots are shaded and there is morning sun for several hours, flowers will bloom right through to mid-autumn. The whole plant is fragrantly scented and the tubular flower petals are full of nectar, making them a magnet for bees. For this reason, bergamot is often called "bee balm". Honey-eating birds are also attracted to the blossoms. Like mint, which is a member of the same family, bergamot has a matted, spreading, root system and does not start shooting upwards until spring.

History and mythology

Bergamot is native to North America and received its botanical name from the sixteenth century Spanish physician, Nicholas Monardez, who first discovered and described it. The leaves, which contain the essential oil thymol, were widely used in an infusion by the Oswego Indians. The herb soon became known to the early American settlers, who called it Oswego Tea, a name which is still popular today. Oil of bergamot, a fragrant essence, does not come from this plant, but from a citrus tree, the bergamot orange, *(Citrus bergamia).* The aromas are similar.

Cultivation

A dressing of well–decayed humus may be applied in spring when the plant begins to shoot upwards. Grass cuttings should be sprinkled over the roots during the hottest part of summer. Bergamot may be grown in clumps as background plants in herb gardens, or in decorative clusters in standard garden beds, the lovely, plush-red, pincushion blooms making splashes of vivid colour. Ours grows in a far-away bed set in a green sward surrounded by a glade of leafy trees. When in bloom, the scarlet flashes draw one from a distance to investigate and admire. A flower is always picked and the honeysuckle-petals tasted for their sweetness. If necessary, lightly tie the slender and rather brittle stems to garden stakes.

Propagation by root division can be done throughout the year. However, the best time is in early spring, when new growth is beginning. The seeds, which are very small, can be sown in a prepared box in spring and planted out when big enough to handle, leaving 15 cm (6 inches) between plants. The fact that bergamot likes to grow in a shady position where the roots can be kept cool and moist, also encourages snails, so be prepared for this by

The Cambridge Scarlet is the best known of the red bergamots and is the type most often used in cooking.

Bergamot can vary in hue from mauve through pink to deep red and is very striking when grown in garden beds. Fresh or dried, this herb is a pleasant addition to a warm bath as it not only has a revitalizing effect but also perfumes the water.

laying a suitable bait nearby, especially when the soft leaves are young. After the plants have finished flowering, cut all stalks back to ground level.

Harvesting and processing

For drying, harvest both foliage and flowers in late summer when the plant is in full bloom and dry them as quickly as possible. Do this by picking the leaves and blooms from the stems and spreading them out on a wire rack in a shady place. When they are dry, store them in airtight containers. Fresh bergamot leaves may be chopped finely, mixed with a little water and frozen in ice cube trays to be used when needed. The flowers may be frozen whole by carefully putting them one by one in an ice cube tray, then gently covering them with water.

Various uses

Culinary

Bergamot leaves go into salads, teas, and cooling summer beverages. Their savoury yet fruity aroma enhances such widely differing foods as vegetables and sweet jellies. They combine well with pork and veal. Fresh or dried, they may be used instead of mint leaves for a change. The flowers can be gently torn apart and added to a tossed green salad.

Medicinal

A herb tea made from bergamot leaves was taken by the Indians and early Americans as a remedy for sore throats, colds and chest complaints.

Cosmetic

Fresh or dried bergamot in a hot bath is revitalising and perfumes the water. An essential oil is made from this plant, both for incense and as a bath oil. The dried flowers and leaves make a fragrant addition to pot-pourri.

Companion planting

Bergamot's attraction for bees makes it an excellent plant to grow near the vegetable garden and in the orchard.

BORAGE

(*Borago officinalis*) *Boraginaceae.*
  Annual.
Propagation: *seeds. All seasons in*
  mild climates. Spring in cold climates.
Position: *semi-shade, sheltered.*
Soil: *average to moist*
Height: *90 cm (3 feet).*
Part used: *leaves, flowers.*

Description

This herb has thick, soft stems and large
leaves, both of which are covered in fine,
bristly hairs. The leaves when fully grown are
approximately 23 cm (9 inches) long, and
15 cm (6 inches) wide. The flowers are star-
shaped and a vivid sky-blue, with an occasional pale pink bloom appearing amongst the
blue. There is also a rare species with white
flowers. The blooms are filled with nectar,
making them an excellent source of food for
bees.

History and mythology

Borage first came from the Middle East. Old
chronicles say that Aleppo was its original
home. Throughout the ages, wherever it was
taken, this plant spread abundantly, adapting
well to almost any soil and climate. The
flowers, with their prominent black anthers
and five-pointed petals of brilliant blue, were
also favourite subjects in the needlework of
past centuries, partly for their simple beauty
and for their association with bravery.

Cultivation

Borage seed germinates so easily that it can be
sown in all seasons in mild climates. In very
cold areas, the best time for cultivating is in
spring, when the oblong, black seeds can be
sown into the open ground into shallow drills,
30 cm (12 inches) apart. Make sure that the
ground has been well turned over first, so that
the soil is reasonably fine. The position for
growing the plants should be moist, with not
too much sun. There should also be shelter
from winds as the main stems, being soft, are
easily broken. Borage is in bloom nearly all
through the year, and is continually seeding
itself, so that once planted, you should never
be without it. It seems to do best when allowed

*The blue borage flowers are a most effective garnish
when floated on the top of drinks or crystallized and
used to decorate sweets and small iced cakes.*

to grow in thick clumps; the plants help to
support each other and the massed effect of the
misty buds and blue flowers is pleasing. If on
the other hand, borage begins to take over the

31

Borage has its origins in the Middle East, but over the centuries it has been introduced into almost every kind of soil and climate, where it readily adapted and became widespread.

garden, it is easily thinned out and the shallow roots dislodged — even when fully grown — by pulling out the stems by hand, remembering that the stalks are prickly.

Harvesting and processing

Borage leaves and flowers may be used fresh at any time of the year. Drying the leaves and flowers is possible, but the method must be quick to prevent spoilage. Take the flowers and leaves off the succulent stalks and place them on wire racks in a shady, airy place. When dry, store them in airtight containers. The flowers may be preserved by crystallizing and used for decorating cakes and trifles. Another method is to freeze them whole by carefully putting them one by one in an ice cube tray and gently covering them with water. When needed, a flowery ice block can be dropped into a glass of fruit juice or any other beverage.

Various uses

Culinary

The young leaves can be very finely chopped, almost minced, and mixed into green salads, or used as fillings, with a little salt and pepper, for sandwiches. Whole young leaves go into punches and wine cups, or they can be dipped in batter, fried, and eaten as a vegetable. Older leaves can be used for soup; these should be finely chopped too. Fresh or dried leaves make

a health-giving tea. The blue flowers can be floated on top of all kinds of drinks and scattered over a green salad just before serving. When crystallized, they decorate cream-swirled sweets and iced cakes. The fresh or dried flowers make a tea.

Medicinal

The branching, leafy plants of borage are rich in potassium, calcium, mineral acids and a very beneficial saline mucilage. It is often mixed with basil to make a delicious herb tea blend. Borage was recommended by Sir Francis Bacon as a heart tonic and by other authorities as a tonic for the adrenal glands and urinary tract. It was looked upon at one time as a herb to engender courage. Borage on its own is also beneficial to the circulation of the blood. Compresses made from the leaves help to relieve congested veins, especially in the legs when a person has been standing for a long time. Borage is related to another healing herb, comfrey.

Cosmetic

A facial steam for dry, sensitive skin may be made with borage leaves and flowers. Borage is also recommended as a tea to help cleanse the skin from the inside by helping to purify the system.

Companion planting

Borage and strawberries are helpful to one another. Because of the sprawling habit of the borage plants, it is advisable to put only a few among the strawberries and the rest outside the beds. Borage will bring bees to the garden.

CARAWAY

(Carum carvi) Umbelliferae. Biennial.

Propagation: *seeds. Spring (again
   in Autumn in mild climates).*
Position: *sheltered, sunny.*
Soil: *average, well drained.*
Height: *60 cm (2 feet).*
Part used: *seeds, roots, fresh leaves
   sometimes.*

Description

Caraway plants grow to 60 cm (2 feet) high,
their foliage is delicate, finely-cut and frond-
like and their white, umbrella-like flowers
bloom in summer. These flowers are followed
by seeds, or fruit, which are brown and
crescent-shaped and are marked with distinc-
tive ridges. The roots are thick and tapering
and are similar in appearance to a small parsnip.

History and mythology

Caraway is indigenous to all parts of Europe
and is also claimed to be native to parts of Asia,
India and North Africa. Its qualities were
recognized by the ancient Egyptians and the
early Greeks and Romans. The herb was
widely known in the Middle Ages and was
popular in Shakespeare's day. Like aniseed,
the fruit has been used for centuries in breads
and cakes and with baked fruit, especially
roast apples. Caraway-seed cake is as traditional in England as apple pie or gingerbread.
The oil expressed from the seeds goes into the
liqueur Kummel. Because caraway was said to
prevent lovers from straying, it was once an
essential ingredient in love potions. The seed,
baked in dough, is given to pet pigeons to keep
them, it is said, from wandering away

Cultivation

Caraway seeds can be sown in spring, and
where the climate is mild, in autumn as well.
Choose a sunny, sheltered position in the
garden and sow the seed in shallow drills,
20 cm (8 inches) apart. When the plants are
about 8 cm (3 inches) high, thin them out to a
distance of 15 cm (6 inches). As the seedlings
do not transplant well, it is not advisable to
start them in seed boxes.

Harvesting and processing

To harvest, when the seeds are about to drop,
cut off all the heads and, like anise seed heads,
dry them on sheets of paper in a shady place,
exposing them to the sun when possible to
completely dry out any moisture. They are
ready to store when the fruit falls away easily
from the shrivelled flower-heads if given a
light shake. Sieve out any pieces of stalk and
pack the seeds into airtight containers. If using
the roots for culinary purposes, they should be
pulled when young. If this is a favourite way
to use your caraway, it is a good idea to make
two sowings, one for the root crop and the
other for the seeds.

Various uses

Culinary

The seeds go with boiled or baked onions
during cooking and into potato dishes.

Sprinkle them into the pot when steaming turnips, beetroot, parsnips, carrots, cabbage and cauliflower. Blend them into cream cheese. Mix them into home-made breads, biscuits and cakes. Shake a few seeds over apples, quinces and pears when baking or stewing them. The roots, when boiled, are eaten like parsnips with a little melted butter or with white sauce. The young leaves go into spring soups and they give a spicy tang to green salads. They give added flavour to certain green vegetables such as spinach, zucchini and marrow.

Medicinal

Caraway's therapeutic and useful qualities as a medicine and in food were known as far back as Biblical times. The ancient Arabs called the seeds *Karawya*. The digestive properties of the fruit are identical with those of aniseed. However, the flavour is stronger and reminiscent of the zesty bite of orange or lemon peel. Caraway seeds and the leaves and root also, are especially good for assisting the activity of the glands and increasing the action of the kidneys.

Cosmetic

As caraway is so good for the digestion, it is probably the reason that Dioscorides, the great Greek physician who lived in the first century A.D., prescribed it for "girls of pale face". Dr Nicholas Culpeper, another famous herbalist, also mentions its digestive and cleansing properties, which are conducive to a clear complexion.

For thousands of years the seeds, leaves and roots of caraway have been used as a natural aid to the digestion and to ensure a clear complexion.

Although caraway is best known for its seeds, in summer it has attractive, umbrella-like blooms.

Companion planting

Caraway and fennel dislike each other, and one hinders the growth of the other. It has been found that caraway grown in heavy soil loosens it and puts the ground in good condition. Caraway is helpful as a feed supplement for increased milk in cows.

CHAMOMILE

Chamomile, English: *(Anthemis nobilis) Compositae. Perennial.*

Chamomile, German: *(Matricaria chamomile) Compositae. Annual.*

Propagation: *seed for both types in Spring. Root division for English chamomile.*

Position: *sunny to semi-shade in hot, dry areas.*

Soil: *light.*

Height: *English Chamomile, creeping ground cover until flowering, then 30 cm (12 inches).*
German Chamomile 45 cm-60 cm (1½-2 feet).

Part used: *flowers.*

(Top) English chamomile
(Bottom) German chamomile

Description

There is a bewildering variety of chamomiles growing wild and in gardens, and superficially many of them look alike, with their finely cut, fern-like leaves and miniature white and gold daisy-heads. (Some may be completely yellow). But on closer inspection there are differences in appearance and foliage colour and their uses are not all the same. The most usual kind found in gardens is the old self-sowing feverfew or febrifuge, a *pyrethrum* which can have either green or golden foliage; it is not used very much today in herbal teas. I was told once that it was considered a cure for headaches and menstrual pain, although German chamomile is a better-known aid for these problems. There is another pyrethrum daisy of the chamomile group with grey foliage and white flowers which is said to be the most effective for pyrethrum insect sprays, many of which are on the market now. Both English and German chamomiles are by far the most popular to grow. The English kind has fine, feathery leaves and a creeping, matting habit. In late summer it sends up stems of flowerheads which make a beautiful informal lawn if kept well watered in a low rain-fall area. The flowers are cut for herb tea, and then the mower, set fairly high, can be run over the plants. Some people have found that this does not make a successful lawn, and there is a hard-to-get variety known as the *Treneague* strain of chamomile which is the very best type for lawns. German chamomile grows quickly into a bushy little plant with fine foliage, and bears flowers profusely for quite some time. The fragrance of chamomile has been likened to fresh apples.

History and mythology

There seems to be some difference of opinion among herbal writers as to which is the "true" chamomile, and which has the most efficacy. *Maythen* was the old Saxon name for English chamomile, (which is also sometimes called Roman chamomile) and the Spaniards called it *manzanilla*, meaning "little apple". The

ancient Egyptians prized it for its curative powers, as did the early Greeks and Romans. It has been used in folk medicine in Britain for centuries. It spreads in its natural state through Europe and the temperate regions of Asia. We saw it growing wild — or what looked very like it — in the ruined beauty of antique Ephesus in Turkey, and all along the roadsides leading to it. Chamomile was a favourite strewing herb on the floors of dwellings for its sweet fresh scent when trodden on and for its insect repellent qualities.

Cultivation

Before planting English or German chamomile seeds in spring, or dividing roots of English chamomile at the same time, work the soil very well if it is heavy, add some sandy loam, dampen the ground and put in the divided roots or seeds. As the seeds are very small, you may prefer to start them off in a prepared seed box. When large enough to handle, plant out the seedlings to about 15 cm (6 inches) apart, and keep them moist until well established. If wanting to make an area for a lawn, plant only English chamomile and keep it well watered in a dry climate. A fixed sprinkler is a good idea. As they begin to creep, a light top dressing, especially in hot weather, will help the plants to mat and spread. Your labour will be re-

Of the many different varieties, English chamomile is one of the most popular for growing in herb gardens. As can be seen from this potted specimen, it has a horizontal growth and delicate foliage.

warded, especially if the plants are allowed to bloom. We recently saw a tiny chamomile lawn, enchanting with its scattering of starry flowers. The unexpected sight gave a magical lift to the spirits and it smelt most sweetly underfoot.

Harvesting and processing

Both English and German chamomile are grown for their flowers, and these should be harvested by midday if possible, before the sun has drawn the valuable volatile essences from the blossoms. Pick the opened heads carefully with scissors on a clear day, and spread them out on a wire sieve, or on sheets of paper, in a cool, airy place. When papery, put the fragrant heads in clean, dry screw-top jars.

Various uses

Culinary

A few whole chamomile flowers are an edible embellishment strewn over a tossed green salad. A pleasant and beneficial beverage to drink at lunch-time, or during the day at any time of the year, may be made with one or two litres of half chamomile tea (sweetened with a little honey to taste) and half natural, sparkling mineral water. Pour into a (glass) jug with ice cubes, thin slices of lemon and a few whole chamomile flowers floating on top.

Medicinal

Chamomile tea has been famous for centuries for its relaxing qualities and the calming of frayed nerves and soothing effect on the digestion. It is helpful to women suffering from menstrual pain and tension. Children also benefit from a mild infusion of this tea if they are restless and overtired. (Even Peter Rabbit was given a soothing cup of chamomile tea by his mother after a narrow escape from Mr. McGregor!). They usually prefer it sweetened with honey, or mixed with peppermint tea. It is a tea for everyone who is suffering from fevers or colds. It is an excellent tea for students studying hard, and for overtired businessmen. An infusion of the flowers, strained and poured into a hot bath, will reduce muscular weariness and fatigue. A well-tried folk remedy for a stye in the eye, is to bathe it frequently with strained, cooled, chamomile tea. We can vouch for its reliability, having tried this cure many times.

Cosmetic

An infusion of chamomile flowers, strained, cooled and used as a hair rinse has been used for centuries to lighten the hair. There are many shampoos, setting lotions and conditioners on the market today containing chamomile, mainly to be used for fair or light brown hair. It benefits the hair at the same time as "blonding" it. Chamomile flowers in sleep pillows mixed with other slumber-inducing herbs (lavender, valerian, hops, roses and lemon verbena) are effective, the warmth of the head releasing the various perfumes to induce relaxation which precedes sleep. Chamomile used in facial steams, or incorporated into cream, is soothing and strengthening to the tissues. It is also used in rejuvenating facial masks, beauty lotions, herbal soap, body lotions, lotions for sunburn, for tired eyes and for aching feet.

Companion planting

Chamomile is an excellent addition to the compost heap, so put spent chamomile tea flowers there as well as any unwanted foliage or plants. When growing, small quantities of chamomile will intensify the oil content in peppermint plants, but if the chamomile increases too much, the peppermint oil will in turn decrease. Small clumps of chamomile growing near onions, cabbages and wheat plants will help them. Chamomile tea has been used to help combat plant diseases. On the farm, calves and other animals with hoof rot are helped by using chamomile in compresses.

German chamomile grows vertically into a small plant and is seen here in a rockery garden.

CHERVIL

(Anthriscus cerefolium) Umbelliferae.
Annual.

Propagation: *seeds. Spring, Autumn.*
Position: *semi-shade, (winter sun if possible).*
Soil: *average, moist.*
Height: *30 cm (12 inches).*
Part used: *leaves.*

Description

Chervil plants grow to 30 cm (12 inches) high and in appearance they resemble parsley, although the fern-like leaves are smaller and finer, the colour is a brighter green and the flavour has a mild taste of aniseed. The white flowers, which appear in early summer, grow in small, flat umbels, and the seeds which follow look rather like caraway seeds, except that they are a little longer and thinner. Chervil is native to Eastern Europe.

History and mythology

Chervil was taken to various countries by the colonizing Romans, who well knew its worth in food and in medicine. On the Continent, chervil soup has been traditional fare for Holy Thursday, as well as being a favoured dish at other times. One authority mentions that chervil was once called *myrrhis* for its volatile oil which has a similar aroma to the resinous substance of *myrrh*.

Cultivation

Chervil is sometimes classed as a biennial, but it is best treated as an annual. The seeds can be sown in spring and autumn in a well prepared garden bed. Never plant them in a seed box, as chervil seedlings are too fragile to transplant. Sow the seeds in shallow drills 30 cm (12 inches) apart, cover them with soil and firm down with the back of a spade. When the seedlings are big enough to handle, thin them out, leaving 10 cm (4 inches) between plants. Keep chervil watered at all times. This herb is frost-tender and in cold areas it needs to grow in a sheltered position. It also dislikes hot, dry conditions, so try and protect the plants from the summer sun. A good idea is to grow chervil under a deciduous tree so that it is shaded

in summer by the leafy boughs, yet is also warmed by the winter sun when the branches are bare. As the plants never grow large, chervil is ideal for cultivation in containers. Select a tub or pot 30 cm (12 inches) in diameter, fill it with a good, porous potting mixture and scatter the seeds over the surface. Press them gently down with a flat piece of board, and lightly sprinkle with water. Keep the pot moist, and when the seedlings are 5 cm (2 inches) high, thin them out to 8 cm (3 inches) between plants.

Harvesting and processing

Chervil can be picked at any time of the year. Break the stems off carefully, taking the outside leaves first, as with parsley, so that the new centre leaves are allowed to grow. If you wish it to self-sow, which it will do readily, do not harvest all the plants when in flower: leave a third to go to seed. The foliage is dried by spreading the sprays out on a wire rack in a cool, airy place away from the light, which will fade the green colour. When brittle, crumble the leaves from the stems and store in airtight containers. Fresh chervil leaves may be chopped finely, mixed with a little water and frozen in ice cube trays to be used when

Densely clustered chervil makes an eye-catching splash of vivid green in a garden. It is also an ideal herb for growing in tubs. But the plants are delicate and dislike extreme heat or cold.

needed. Chervil butter, made by pounding chopped chervil leaves into softened butter, then cutting into squares when cold, may also be frozen in sealed polythene bags.

Various uses

Culinary

Chervil is one of the four fragrant herbs which make up the delicate bouquet, "fines herbes", the others being chives, tarragon and parsley in equal parts and all finely chopped. Chervil's soft leaves make it indispensable for sprinkling over food when cut up finely, both as a garnish and a flavouring. Sometimes whole sprays may be used for garnishing. Chervil should never be cooked for more than ten to fifteen minutes, otherwise the fine flavour will be lost. Use this herb in chervil soup and in many types of sauces. Fold into scrambled eggs, omelettes, creamed potatoes and cream cheese. Sprinkle it liberally on salads and use it as a filling for sandwiches. Chervil goes with poultry and fish and is excellent sprinkled on cooked, crisp vegetables with a little melted butter and freshly ground pepper and salt.

Medicinal

Chervil has been traditionally valued as a blood purifier and for this reason it was widely eaten in the spring. It was known to help the kidneys and was taken to ease rheumatic conditions. Externally, a poultice of the leaves helped disperse swellings and bruises. Dr Nicholas Culpeper advises in his *Complete Herbal* that "The garden chervil being eaten, doth moderately warm the stomach...".

Cosmetic

Chervil's cosmetic value lies in its cleansing properties as a blood purifier, thus paving the way for a clear and healthy complexion.

Companion planting

Chervil and radishes help each other in companion planting, radishes growing near chervil having a hotter taste. It has been reported that a steeped tea made from equal parts of chamomile, chervil and lemon balm, applied in a compress, is helpful in curing hoof rot in animals. Chervil is one of many aromatic herbs that aid the vegetable garden when grown amongst it.

CHICORY

(Cichorum intybus) Compositae.
Perennial.

Propagation: *seeds. Spring.*
Position: *sunny.*
Soil: *average, well drained.*
Height: *1.80m (6 feet).*
Part used: *leaves, roots (in coffee).*

Description

Chicory is one of the taller herbs. The lower leaves are broad and long like spinach leaves, while the higher leaves are smaller and sparser and grow on many branching stalks. The large, daisy-like flowers are pale blue and grow in clusters of two or three along the stalks. They close about noon, except in dull weather when they stay fully open all day. The leaves have a very bitter taste, and for eating in any quantity, are much more palatable when they have been cultivated by forcing and blanching in the dark.

History and mythology

Chicory was known to the civilizations of the ancient world. Arabian physicians used it and we know the Romans valued it by the writings of Pliny and others. For many centuries it has been found growing wild in different parts of Europe and it is known by different names in different countries. The old English name for it was succory. It is also known on the Continent as witloof and Belgian endive. In England it was a favourite ingredient in love philtres.

Cultivation

For growing in the garden, plant the seeds in spring in a prepared bed where they are to remain, in drills 25 mm (1 inch) deep and 30 cm (12 inches) apart. Keep the ground watered until the shoots appear, and watch for snails and caterpillars. For blanching, the number of roots required are dug out. This should be possible six months after planting, and takes place in the autumn. The foliage is cut off and the roots are then stood upright, close together, in a deep box or pot, with a covering of light, sandy soil 15 cm (6 inches) above the top of the roots. They must be kept in a moist, dark place such as a glass house or warm shed. As they grow, the new young leaves become elongated and blanched. But if there is not enough darkness the foliage turns green and this results in excessive bitterness. As soon as the white leaves show above the soil the plants are ready for lifting. The root is then cut away, leaving sufficient at the base to hold the folded leaves together. The chicory now looks like an elongated lettuce heart of creamy coloured leaves, the outside ones measuring approximately 15 cm (6 inches) long. It is important to use the chicory as soon as possible as it deteriorates quickly.

Harvesting and processing

Leaves for herb tea may be picked from their stalks and laid on wire racks until dry, then crumbled and stored in airtight containers. The procedure for drying, roasting, and grinding chicory roots is usually carried out by manufacturers with kiln-drying equipment. Large quantities of the plants are cultivated on the Continent for this, as ground

Chicory is a tall-growing herb with clusters of pale blue flowers along its stems. Its old English name was succory and it was used in love potions.

chicory root sometimes forms an ingredient in or adulteration to coffee. It does not contain caffeine.

Various uses

Culinary

When chicory has been cultivated for blanching, it is classed as a vegetable and there are many different methods of cooking it. It may also be eaten raw in salads, the texture of the leaves being smooth and fine and the flavour just a little on the bitter side. When left to grow wild in the garden, the new young

This young chicory plant is at the best stage for eating, when the flavour is more delicate and subtle.

leaves are best to use, as they are not as strong-tasting as the older ones. Tear up a few young leaves and add them to a green salad.

Medicinal

The leaves have excellent medicinal qualities, being helpful to the functions of the liver and gall. Chicory roots when roasted and ground can be made into a health-giving beverage which has been given to people suffering from bilious attacks and constipation. However, it is not supposed to be good for those who are anaemic.

Cosmetic

As both leaves and roots of chicory are such an excellent liver tonic, any tendency to yellowness of skin and eyes should clear as bodily functions improve.

Companion planting

Chicory greens make an excellent fodder for some animals, including sheep, cows and horses. A few leaves mixed with our son's horse's feed, helped keep its general condition good.

CHIVES

Chives, Onion: *(Allium schoenoprasum) Liliaceae. Perennial.*
Chives, Garlic: *(A. tuberosum) Liliaceae. Perennial.*
Propagation: *seeds, division of bulbs. Spring, (Autumn in mild climates).*
Position: *sunny, open.*
Soil: *fairly rich, well drained.*
Height: *onion chives, 30 cm (12 inches); garlic chives, 60 cm (2 feet).*
Part used: *leaves.*

Description

Onion chives, when young, resemble tufts of fine grass. As they mature the leaves become circular and hollow with a distinct taste of onion. The mauve flowers, which appear in summer, are made up of thick knots of cylindrical petals forming round heads like clover blossoms.

Garlic chives, or Chinese chives as they are sometimes called, look very much like onion chives when they are young, but as they mature the leaves become broad and flat, the colour is a light green and the flavour is characteristic of garlic, but much milder. The flowers begin to bloom in summer, in white, star-like clusters at the top of long, round stems which are strong and tough and not suitable for eating.

History and mythology

Chives belong to the same family as garlic, shallot and leek and are thought to be a native of Britain. They grow wild in rocky pastures in the temperate areas of northern Europe. It is thought that they were known by the Ancients, as they grow wild in Greece and Italy. The old French name was *petit poureau* because of their rush-like appearance. Dr Nicholas Culpeper, in his *Complete Herbal,* says that chives are under the dominion of Mars, and are hot and dry in the fourth degree sending "very hurtful vapours to the brain".

Cultivation

All chives can be raised easily from seed in

(Left) Onion chives
(Right) Garlic chives

spring, when planted in shallow drills in a box containing fine soil. Autumn sowing is also possible where the winters are mild. When seedlings have passed the stage where they look like delicate grass, plant them out into the garden, or into 15 cm (6 inch) pots for the kitchen window sill. Chives form a small bulb, so when planting them, allow about twelve bulbs to a clump, keeping the clumps 30 cm (12 inches) apart. Both onion and garlic chives are attacked by aphis, which usually can be eliminated, first by watering the leaves, then applying Derris Dust liberally to the wet foliage. This should be carried out at least twice a week until the pests have gone. In winter, the tops of chives wither back, then in spring they begin to shoot again. This is the best time to divide the clumps, making sure they are no larger than 5 cm (2 inches) in diameter. It is very important not to let the bunch of chives get too large as the centre will then die out, owing to lack of nourishment. Chives can also disappear if allowed to flower profusely, thereby exhausting the plants. So pick off flower buds as they appear. You will

Onion chives have attractive mauve flowers, but these should be removed to ensure healthy plants.

The flowers of garlic chives are white and grow on tough stems which are not suitable for eating.

be rewarded with healthy plants if they are watered well and if a little decayed manure is dug into the soil occasionally. When gathering chives, do not cut the leaves with scissors, as this causes them to die back slightly leaving an unattractive brown edge. Always pick off the leaves at the base with your fingers.

Harvesting and processing

Drying chives in the normal way, either in bunches on a wire rack, or in the oven, is not satisfactory as they lose their colour and flavour. The chives that one sees in food stores in bottles are dried by the "freeze dry" method. Fresh chives, both onion and garlic flavoured, may be chopped finely, mixed with a little water and frozen in ice cube trays to be used when needed. Chive butter made by mashing chopped chives into softened butter, allowing to set in the refrigerator, then cutting into squares, may also be frozen in sealed polythene bags.

Various uses

Culinary

Onion chives are an excellent standby for giving a subtle flavour to food when onions themselves may be too strong and indigestible. This is because there is not as much sulphur in the composition of chives — in spite of what Dr Culpeper said. Garlic chives are used instead of garlic for the same reason. The classic blend of delicately flavoured herbs known as "fines herbes" consists of onion chives, chervil, parsley and tarragon. These herbs are finely chopped and mixed together in equal quantities making a deliciously savoury yet mild blend, to flavour and garnish omelettes, cooked chicken and fish, salads, steamed vegetables, soups and mornays. The flavour of both onion and garlic chives is destroyed with long cooking, so if using them in hot food, add them during the last five to ten minutes. Finely chopped chives go into all kinds of salads, egg dishes, cream cheese, fish and poultry mornays, savoury sauces and mayonnaise. Chopped chives make an attractive and tasty garnish.

Medicinal

Like the onion family, to which chives belong, they contain a pungent volatile oil with some sulphur present. Chives stimulate the appetite, have a tonic effect on the kidneys and are said to help to lower high blood pressure.

Cosmetic

Chives, amongst many other herbs, are a source of calcium which helps strengthen the nails and teeth, always an important factor in achieving natural beauty.

Companion planting

Chives growing near the roots of apple trees which are infested with scab have helped reduce the scab. A chive tea made into a spray has been helpful in combating downy and powdery mildew on gooseberries and cucumbers. Chives also have a beneficial effect on carrots when grown near them. The carrots grow larger than usual. It has also been reported that chives are beneficial when cut up and mixed with the feed of very young turkeys. These findings only apply to onion chives.

COMFREY

*(Symphytum officinale) Boraginaceae.
Perennial.*

Propagation: *seeds, root division.
Spring (again Autumn in temperate
climates).*
Position: *shady.*
Soil: *average, moist.*
Height: *1.20m (4 feet).*
Part used: *leaves, roots.*

Description

There are several varieties of comfrey, the
most common being the *officinale*, the kind
described here. Comfrey belongs to the same
family as borage, and there is a similarity in
their appearance, although the hairs covering
comfrey's stalks and foliage are much finer
than the rough bristles of borage. Comfrey
grows to 1.20 m (4 feet) high, and is perennial.
A thick-set, bushy plant, the outside leaves
can measure 60 m (2 feet) long and 20 cm (8
inches) wide. The mauve flowers droop in
bell-like clusters at the tip of the plant and are
in bloom for most of the summer.

History and mythology

Comfrey originally came from Europe and
Asia. A variety known as Prickly Comfrey
was highly regarded in the Caucasus as a
fodder plant for animals. Historically it
has been known amongst country folk for
hundreds of years as a wound-healing plant,
and in the Middle Ages was a well known
remedy for broken bones. Gerard, a famous
herbalist of a bygone age, wrote: "A salve
concocted from the fresh herb will certainly
tend to promote the healing of bruised and
broken parts."

Cultivation

For propagating, sow the seeds in spring —
and again in autumn where the climate is
temperate — in a well-prepared bed, preferably under spreading trees. Keep moist while
the seeds are germinating. When the plants are
a few centimetres high, thin them out. Watch
particularly for snails and caterpillars, which,
if not controlled, can shred the leaves of even
fully-grown plants to a fine lace. Increasing by
root division is carried out in autumn, leaving
at least 60 cm (2 feet) each way when planting.
The roots are persistent and any little piece left
in the soil will shoot.

Harvesting and processing

Comfrey roots and leaves should be harvested
as required, as they are more effective when
fresh. If this is not possible and drying is
desired, select unblemished leaves, lay them
flat on racks, or on sheets of paper, in an airy
place until crisp, then crumble them coarsely
and pack into airtight containers. For the
roots, dig the required amount for storage,
wash and dry out in an airy place.

Various uses

Culinary

Herbalists maintain that comfrey leaves are wholesome as a food. The large, outside foliage is rather coarse, so pluck only the succulent, young leaves which have a cucumber taste and a delicious texture. Coat the young leaves in batter and fry them in oil, dust with salt and pepper and serve as a vegetable. Gently steam the chopped leaves and eat them like spinach, or add a few chopped leaves to spinach during cooking. Put some leaves into the juice extractor together with any vegetable for an extra nutritious drink.

Medicinal

The leaves and roots of comfrey have long been a country remedy for sprains, bruises and wounds when made into poultices and applied to the affected parts. An infusion of the leaves or roots has been given successfully for chest colds, for the circulation and for the intestines. The old name of "knit bone" or "boneset" was given to comfrey because it helps broken bones to mend more quickly. We have a skiing friend who applied comfrey poultices to a broken limb (he drank the tea as well) and to the astonishment of the doctors, his recovery was hastened by six months. The leaves and

For centuries comfrey has been a folk remedy for all kinds of injuries, including sprains and broken bones. It also has a reputation as a very wholesome and nutritious food and can be eaten as a vegetable.

roots are rich in mucilage — a glutinous substance. They also contain a beneficial element called allantoin, as well as tannin and some starch.

Cosmetic

Comfrey cream, or comfrey ointment, is soothing and healing for the skin, and is especially helpful when applied overnight for wrinkles under the eyes. Comfrey tea helps cleanse the blood stream and clear the complexion. Comfrey leaves in a facial steam help tired and ageing skins.

Companion planting

Comfrey is closely related to borage, and is helpful in much the same way if a few plants are grown near a strawberry bed to improve the size and flavour of the berries. Comfrey leaves are an excellent addition to the compost heap. A liquid fertilizer made from large, old comfrey leaves which have been left to rot in water — and then broken down with more water and applied to the roots of plants has been found helpful *(Esther Deans' Gardening Book)*.

CORIANDER

(Coriandrum sativum) Umbelliferae.
  Annual.

Propagation: *seeds. Spring (again in*
  Autumn in temperate climates).
Position: *sunny, sheltered.*
Soil: *light, well drained.*
Height: *45 cm-60 cm (1½-2 feet).*
Part used: *leaves, seeds.*

Description

Coriander has lacy, feathery foliage with a
unique, strong aroma quite different from the
other herbs it resembles so closely in appearance, such as anise, caraway, dill and fennel,
all of whose leaves have, in varying degrees of
pungency, a warm spicy anise-scent. A mixture of lemon peel and sage is one description
of the flavour of fresh coriander leaves. The
mauve-tinted white blossoms appear in summer in frothy profusion, followed by fruit,
which, when green and unripened, have an
even stronger scent than the foliage. In fact,
the name coriander is derived from the Greek
koris, which means bug: the soft green seeds
do smell exactly like an emerald-coloured,
odoriferous insect which infests citrus trees.
When the small, oval coriander seeds have
hardened and ripened to a pale fawn colour,
they are one of the most deliciously fragrant of
all spices used in cooking. Fresh coriander is
sometimes known as Chinese parsley.

History and mythology

Coriander grew first in southern Europe, and
centuries ago found its way to many other
countries. The Romans introduced it to Britain; it also found its way to India, the Middle
East, China and Peru, to name some of the
lands where it has become a favourite herb.
The Egyptians made use of it in ancient days,
and for the Hebrews it was one of the bitter
herbs used at the Feast of the Passover. In the
Bible the seed is likened to manna, tasting
"like wafers made with honey". (Exodus
16:31).
  History records that it grew in the Hanging
Gardens of Babylon. The Chinese believed
that the seeds contained the power of immor-
tality. The whole seed was once popular in
confectionary and provided the centres of
rainbow balls.

Cultivation

Before planting the seed, choose a position
which is both sunny and sheltered, as the
young plants need protection from prevailing
winds to prevent them from falling over.
Work the soil until it is fine and crumbly,
adding a little lime if the ground is acid.
Incidentally, coriander seed remains fertile for
five to seven years. Sow the seeds in spring
(and again in autumn in temperate zones)
directly into the ground in 12 mm (½ inch)
deep drills, 30 cm (12 inches) apart. Cover and
pack the soil down well, then keep moist until
the seedlings appear. Water regularly in hot,
dry weather, preferably in the late afternoon
or evening so as not to scorch the plants. As
they grow, they may need tying to thin bam-
boo or wooden stakes.

Harvesting and processing

Fresh coriander leaves may be picked at any time during the growing period. For drying, spread leaf sprays on sieves in a warm, airy place, and when crisp, crumble the leaves from the stalks and store in airtight containers. For freezing, the ice-cube method is not recommended, owing to the strong odour of the foliage. It is better to parcel up freshly washed sprays in foil, folding the edges firmly, and then put them into the freezer where they will keep for several weeks. To harvest the seeds, cut off all the heads when they are about to drop, and like ripe anise, dry them on sheets of paper in a shady place, exposing them to the sun when possible. They are ready to store when the fruit falls away from the shrivelled flower-heads if given a light shake. Sieve out any pieces of stalks, and pack the seeds into airtight containers.

Various uses

Culinary

The leaves are not used extensively in food, but are very popular in certain regional dishes. You will find coriander leaves in Egyptian, Mediterranean, Oriental and Indian cooking. We tasted it once in a French Restaurant, employed discreetly in a simple chicken dish, giving it a hauntingly delicious flavour. The fresh leaves garnish curries, rice and other ethnic dishes, and once you become used to the flavour, your palate will tell you when to add it for a piquant, individual touch. The seeds are used far more frequently, and when whole, contribute to other spices in a pickling blend. The ground seed flavours fish, poultry and meat dishes. It is a useful spice in fruit cakes, gingerbread, biscuits, pastries and bread. The ground seed is also excellent sprinkled over apples, pears and peaches while baking. A pinch flavours eggplant, zucchini and capsicums. Ground coriander seed is a necessary ingredient when mixing a curry blend or a mixed spice blend.

Medicinal

Hippocrates and other Greek physicians employed coriander in their medicines. The digestive action of the seed is particularly effective with carbohydrates and has been used traditionally, whole or ground, in breads and cakes. Coriander's use in cornbread, or polenta, goes back to the early Romans. Coriander water (like dill water) was used to

Coriander, also known as Chinese parsley, has delicate, feathery foliage and in summer it flowers profusely.

ease windy colic. The ground seed, or fluid extract, was often incorporated into laxatives to help make them more palatable, and to prevent griping. Coriander seed, crushed and inhaled, will relieve dizziness. Because of this, it was once called "dizzycorn". It was among plants mentioned in the *Medical Papyrus of Thebes* written in 1552 B.C. Coriander was also believed to be good for purifying the blood and was frequently prescribed for kidney stones and other urinary disfunctions. European cultures recommend a tea infusion or a soup of coriander leaves and barley water as a tonic-stimulant for convalescents. Ancient Egyptians over 3000 years ago placed sprigs of fresh coriander in tombs to protect the souls on future journeys.

Companion planting

Coriander when grown near anise helps anise seeds to germinate and to grow into bigger, healthier plants. On the other hand, coriander has the opposite effect on fennel and will hinder germination of the seeds. It has been noted that coriander likes the company of chervil; they make good companion plants. Honey bees are attracted to coriander flowers.

CRESS

Cress, Water: *(Nastertium officinale)*
 Cruciferae. Perennial.
Cress, Land: *(Lepidium sativatum)*
 Cruciferae. Annual.
Propagation: *seeds. Spring, Autumn.*
Position: *semi-shade.*
Soil: *loamy for all cresses. Water cress
 in watery conditions.*
Height: *water cress 45 cm (1½ feet)
 land cress 15 cm (6 inches).*
Part used: *leaves.*

Description

Cress is native to Europe and parts of Asia. We
have mentioned several types of cresses,
because it is often believed that the only one
that grows is water cress, and then only in
a stream. However, it can be grown successfully in soil, as long as it is kept damp and
shady. All cresses have a peppery flavour.

Water cress has a creeping habit, the stalks are
sappy and hollow, the small leaves are almost
round and the tiny flowers are white.

*(Top) American
 upland cress*
(Bottom) Water cress

Land cress has three types, all of which can be
grown in the garden or on sprouting trays,
and which we can recommend. Their popular
names are curled cress, American upland cress
and French cress. They are all annuals. Curled
cress, when growing, looks like a fleshy-
leaved parsley. The leaves are light green and
the flavour is hot and sharp. American upland
cress has jaggedly cut green leaves which
grow from the centre of the plant in thick,
round layers. The flavour of this cress is typi-
cally hot. French cress differs again in appearance. The leaves are pale green with a ruffled
edge and their texture is fine. This cress grows
in small clumps.

History and mythology

Water cress is described in an early Anglo-
Saxon herbal as being one of nine sacred herbs
included in a chant sung by magicians to repel
evil, especially the "loathed flying venom".
The song is thought originally to have been a
heathen lay of great antiquity. The name for
water cress was "stime".

Cultivation

Water cress needs water as well as soil for
growing. The water must not be stagnant, so
if there is no running stream nearby, try a
shallow trough for water cress. Start by sowing seeds in a prepared box in spring or
autumn. When the seedlings are big enough,
transfer them to the trough, which is half filled
with loamy soil. Place the trough under a tap
in semi-shade, and as the seedlings grow,
gradually fill the trough with water, tipping it
away carefully about once a week and refilling
with water. The more cress is cut, the more it
will branch. In summer, close cutting will
prevent flowering.

The land cresses are all cultivated in the
same way. Sow the seed in shallow furrows
straight into the garden in prepared soil, cover
and water well. As germination is rapid, the
plants are ready for picking within a short
time. Curled cress can be sown repeatedly
throughout the year. Where winters are
severe, do not sow once the frost starts. Water
the plants in dry weather and if the soil is poor,
dig in a little fertilizer from time to time. The
best position is in semi-shade, although plants
will grow in full sun if they are kept watered.

There are commercial packages now on the

American upland cress has serrated leaves and small, yellow flowers. The flavour is distinctively hot.

Water cress grows naturally in flowing water, but it can also be successfully raised in a trough if kept in semi-shade and regularly given plenty of water.

market containing seeds and trays, which are excellent for growing cress indoors. When grown without soil, the cress is ready for cutting before it matures into a fully-grown plant. The type of cress used is the choice of the manufacturer and is usually accompanied by mustard, its traditional companion.

Harvesting and processing

Cress is a difficult herb to dry for culinary use as its main contribution to a dish is its fresh flavour and appearance. For herb teas, water cress leaves may be dried on an airy rack, and when crisp, crumbled into airtight containers. Any of the cresses may be chopped finely, mixed with a little water and deep frozen in ice cube trays for use in flavouring soups and stews when added at the end of cooking time. Sprigs of cress may be wrapped in foil, sealed and kept in the deep freeze for some weeks.

Various uses

Culinary

Cress leaves are invaluable in salads. They are excellent for garnishing. Cress sandwiches are delicious. Cress soup has an unusual and excellent flavour as well as being healthful. If you have enough cress, use it instead of spinach in a quiche.

Medicinal

All cresses are rich in vitamins and minerals and contain sulphur, iron, iodine and phosphorous. They are a natural blood purifier and are said to clear the complexion and brighten the eyes. Cress soup or "pottage" according to Dr Culpeper was: "A good remedy to cleanse the blood in the spring, and helps head-aches . . .".

Cosmetic

As mentioned, cresses abound in vitamins and trace elements which are essential for maintaining a healthy body. If taken regularly in the form of tea, soup, or raw in salads, they clear the complexion, bring a sparkle to the eyes and help to prevent hair from falling out.

DILL

(Anethum graveolens) Umbelliferae.
  Annual.

Propagation: *seeds. Spring, Autumn.*
Position: *sunny, sheltered.*
Soil: *light, well drained.*
Height: *90 cm (3 feet).*
Part used: *seeds, leaves.*

Description

Dill is similar to fennel in appearance, although it is a smaller plant. It has plumes of dark green leaves and pale yellow flowerheads which form oval, flat fruit or seeds in abundance in late summer and autumn.

History and mythology

Dill is native to the Mediterranean countries and to southern Russia. Once it was renowned for warding off evil spells:

> "Here holy Vervain, and here Dill,
> Gainst witchcraft much availing."

I once read that in America, dill and fennel seed were known as "meetin' seed", having been given to children to eat during long Sunday sermons.

Cultivation

As dill seedlings are soft and delicate, they do not transplant easily, therefore sow in spring and autumn (where winters are not too severe) in a prepared bed, where they are to remain. The slender central stems are easily flattened by strong winds, so seedlings are best grown in a sheltered position and with as much sun as possible. If the soil is sour, lime it well before sowing the seeds in shallow drills 25 cm (10 inches) apart. Firm down the soil after covering and water well. During the summer, several sowings can be made for a continuous supply of leaves. If leaves are picked from the centre, the setting of flowers will be delayed.

Harvesting and processing

The seeds ripen in autumn and can be collected as soon as the first few fall. Snip off the heads and spread them out on a tray in the sun for a few days. When they are completely dry, the seeds shake out easily from the heads. They should then be stored in airtight containers.

If wishing to re-sow dill seed, it should be done within three years for good germinating results. When drying the aromatic, anise-tasting foliage, to retain maximum flavour, start cutting the leafy stalks before the flowerheads appear. Then spread out the frond-like leaves on a wire rack in a shady, cool place. When dry, the leaves are rubbed away from their stalks and kept sealed until needed. For freezing, chop the fresh leaves finely, mix with a little water and put into ice cube trays in the freezer. Sprays of fresh dill may be wrapped in foil, sealed and kept in the deep freeze for some weeks.

Various uses

Culinary

Dill seed flavours and helps the digestion of steamed cabbage, coleslaw, sauerkraut, cucumbers, onions, various chutneys and

pickles, pastries, breads, sauces and cooked root vegetables.

The finely chopped leaves go with almost all foods, as their flavour is pleasing to most palates. Try mixing a little into cottage or cream cheese. Sprinkle some over omelettes while cooking. Stir a spoonful into white sauce and into salad dressings. Use them lavishly in green salads; mix them through a potato salad and sprinkle them over thinly sliced cucumber. Spread them quite thickly over lamb, veal, or chicken while roasting and add a little more to the gravy. Dill leaves are an excellent flavouring for fish, shellfish, rice and egg dishes. Sprinkle them over cooked, buttered vegetables as a tasty garnish and use them in the same way for soup. Dill soup is delicious. A few whole fronds of green dill make an attractive embellishment as a change from parsley.

Medicinal

Dill's reputation as a soothing herb was well known to the ancient world, particularly to the early Norse peoples of Scandinavia. The name stems from the Norse word *dilla* meaning "to lull". The medicinal value of this plant

Dill seedlings are very fragile and do not transplant easily. They should not be planted in seed boxes but put straight into prepared beds, where they are to remain. Young plants need protection from the wind.

lies in the seeds, which are rich in oils with beneficial digestive properties, thus helping the assimilation of food and dispelling flatulence. In cooking, both the seeds and leaves with their spicy flavour are used, although the foliage does not possess the same concentration of oil as the seeds.

Cosmetic

Dill is said to have properties which strengthen the fingernails. The Greeks and Romans used oil distilled from dill for essence and for perfume.

Companion planting

Cabbage plants are especially aided by dill growing nearby. Dill also helps corn, lettuce and cucumber plants. When in flower, dill attracts honey bees to the garden. Dill, together with fennel and caraway as a feed supplement, helps increase the milk supply in cows and goats.

FENNEL, FLORENCE

(Foeniculum vulgare dulce)
Umbelliferae. Annual.

Propagation: *seeds. Spring, Autumn.*
Position: *sunny.*
Soil: *well drained, medium to light.*
Height: *90 cm (3 feet).*
Part used: *swollen stem base,*
foliage, seeds.

Description

The fennel mentioned here must not be confused with the wild fennel *(F. vulgare)*, which is a tall-growing perennial that does not produce the swollen stem base of the annual variety. Perennial fennel is usually found growing wild in low-lying places that are subject to flooding and also along roadside banks and ditches. It is often wrongly referred to as aniseed because of a similarity in flavour and appearance, (see page 20 for a description of anise). Florence fennel is recommended for the home gardener because of its many uses in the kitchen: stem base, foliage and seeds all being valuable in different ways. The foliage is feathery and light green in colour, the bright yellow flower-umbels bloom in summer and are followed in early autumn by seeds of pale green that dry to a light biscuit colour.

History and mythology

Although fennel is a native of the Mediterranean lands, its origins are shrouded in mystical legends and the wondrous properties of the leaves and especially the seeds, are found in the folklore of many countries. It was certainly one of the good "magical" herbs, a sure defence against all evil. In Greek mythology, Prometheus concealed the fire of the sun in a hollow fennel stalk and brought it down to earth from heaven for the human race. Pliny declares that the herb enables the eye to perceive with clarity the beauty of nature.

Cultivation

If growing Florence fennel for the swollen stems, sow the seed in late spring or early summer, straight into the ground, where plants are to remain, in rows of shallow drills that are 30 cm (12 inches) apart, the seedlings to be thinned out later to 20 cm (8 inches) apart. The seed bed should be well dug, then limed and manured if necessary. A rich soil will give best results. Autumn sowing can be done as well if the climate is not too severe, and the thickened stem base should be ready to use in early spring. For a sizeable base and to give the foliage a good colour, fennel requires plenty of water during dry periods. When the base has swollen to the size of a golf ball, cover it with earth, continually adding more to keep the bulb covered as it swells. Remove the flower-heads as they appear. After about fourteen days, the swollen base or bulb will be large enough to use. Cut each one away from the roots, tie them together by the foliage and hang in a dry place until required. Florence fennel bulbs are seen hanging like this in greengrocer shops where they are usually

52

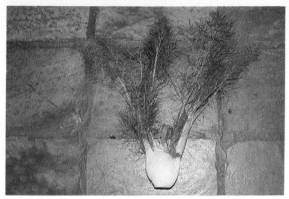

The bulb-like base of Florence fennel can be sliced and added to a salad or cooked as a vegetable.

Florence fennel, here growing with garlic chives, is the type best recommended for use in the kitchen.

referred to as finocchio. It is advisable to use the bulbs within 10 days after cutting, otherwise the fresh, crisp texture is lost.

Harvesting and processing

Unlike dill, the drying of the foliage is not recommended. It is a little too sappy for success and by the time it has dried, most of the flavour has been lost. For freezing, chop the fresh leaves finely, mix with a little water and put into ice cube trays in the freezer. Sprigs of fresh fennel may be wrapped in foil, sealed and kept in the deep freeze for some weeks. If wishing to dry the heads for the seeds, allow them to ripen in autumn, then treat them in the same way as dill — that is, clip off the heads, sun-dry for a few days, then shake out all the seeds and store them in airtight containers.

Various uses

Culinary

Fennel seeds, whole or ground, help to digest starchy foods such as bread, pastries, biscuits and pasta. They assist the assimilation of cabbage, Brussels sprouts, broccoli, cauliflower and onions, as well as many root vegetables. Fennel leaves can be chopped and used sparingly to flavour and help digest potato salad, green salad, spaghetti sauce and rice. Use with fish while cooking. In fact, the leaves are traditional with fish, and if baking a whole fish,

branches of the foliage make a fragrant bed for it to rest on during cooking. The swollen base can be cut into thin rings and separated like an onion for salads; or the base can be cut in half and cooked as a vegetable and served with a plain white sauce, or a cheese sauce.

Medicinal

Fennel has always had a reputation for helping the eyesight (and some say second-sight also). Fennel seed tea is still used by many for bathing sore eyes. The tea also relieves flatulence and for hundreds of years has been recommended for those who wish to lose weight.

Cosmetic

Fennel seed has traditionally been used in home beauty preparations and is said to smooth lines away. Fennel seed made into a strong infusion (or tea) is blended with honey and buttermilk for a cleansing lotion. A mild infusion of fennel seed makes an excellent skin freshener. Allow it to cool before using. The same infusion refreshes tired eyes when pads of cotton wool which have been soaked in the liquid are placed on the eyelids for about five minutes. I have made a revitalizing face mask with a combination of a strong fennel seed infusion, honey and yoghurt stirred together then spread on the face and neck. It should be left for fifteen minutes while you lie down, then gently rinsed off with cool water.

Companion planting

Fennel does not help caraway, tomatoes, kohlrabi or dwarf beans. Fennel and coriander do not grow well together, coriander inhibiting the formation of fennel seed. Do not plant fennel and wormwood together either, as wormwood stunts the growth of fennel plants. Like dill, fennel as a feed supplement for cows and goats will increase their milk supply. Fennel repels fleas.

53

GARLIC

(Allium sativum) Liliaceae. Perennial.

Propagation: *segments of bulbs.*
   Spring.
Position: *sunny.*
Soil: *well drained.*
Height: *90 cm (3 feet).*
Part used: *bulb.*

Description

Garlic grows into a tall, 90 cm (3 feet) high plant with long, flat leaves measuring approximately 25 mm (1 inch) across and 30 cm (12 inches) long. From the centre of the plant a willowy, round flower-stalk thrusts upwards above the greyish leaves, the flower that appears being a compact collection of mauve-tinted white petals. These blossoms, either fresh or dried, are sometimes used in floral arrangements.

History and mythology

Garlic has been known for so many thousands of years that its origins are rather obscure. It is thought to have come first from south-eastern Siberia, from whence it spread to the Mediterranean countries where it became naturalized. It was known in antiquity, Homer having mentioned it several times. Other classic writers who recorded it were Pliny, Virgil and Horace, and later, Chaucer and Shakespeare. Garlic was included in the diet of the ancient Egyptians, Romans and Greeks and the knowledge of its excellent qualities circulated down through the centuries and into different countries.

Cultivation

Mature garlic bulbs are made up of tightly clustered bulblets or cloves, each being sheathed in a pearly, papery skin. The whole bulb is "tissue-wrapped" by nature in the same type of covering, which must be removed so that the bulbs can be broken away from each other. For planting purposes, do not remove the skin from the cloves themselves. Spring is the best time for growing garlic. Separate the bulblets, and keeping them upright with the root-end downwards,

press them into drills 5 cm (2 inches) deep into soil which has previously been dug deeply and thoroughly turned over — with the addition of well-decayed manure if the ground is poor. Keep the cloves 15 cm (6 inches) apart, cover them with soil and water well. Soon the spear-like, grey-green leaves appear, then come the flower-stalks, each with a long, swelling bud at the end. As the stalks lengthen and the buds grow plumper, they eventually burst into flower.

Harvesting and processing

Harvesting of the bulbs usually takes place about six months after planting the cloves, when the flowers are fading and the leaves are yellowing and beginning to shrivel. Dig the bulbs, shake them free of dirt and plait several together with the remaining leaves. Hang the plaited garlic in a dry place where air is circulating. If the bulbs are exposed to a moist atmosphere they will mildew. When the bulbs have hardened, any remnants of foliage can be cut away and the knobs stored in a dry and airy container, such as an open-weave basket, until needed.

Various uses

Culinary

Garlic is indispensable in many types of cooking. Not only does it impart its own unique aroma, thus heightening the taste and savour of the dish, but it aids the digestion as well. Before using the bulblets, or cloves, for eating, their transparent skin should be peeled away. There are many who feel that garlic is an acquired taste, and prefer only the merest whiff of the bulb's pungent scent. Therefore it is more acceptable for them to rub a salad bowl, a saucepan, or a casserole dish with a cut clove of garlic, rather than to use whole cloves in their food. Eventually, if, and when, one becomes addicted, the amount of garlic may be increased gradually until the ideal quantity for each person is reached. There are others who can never have enough garlic, and for them one of the most delicious foods is *aioli,* originating from provincial France. It is a thick, strong-tasting, golden mayonnaise made with eggs, olive oil and crushed garlic, to be eaten with peeled, boiled potatoes and mopped up with bread, or served together with a bowl of shelled hard-boiled eggs, or to have as a sauce to accompany globe artichoke, avocados, asparagus, boiled fish, steamed chicken or snails — the combinations are many and varied (recipe page 106). In any case, garlic is accepted as a universal flavouring, whether in recognizable quantities, or in discreet amounts. It is known in the dishes of the Mediterranean countries. It goes with lamb, pork, veal, beef, tomatoes, eggplant, zucchini, in curries, in Chinese cooking, in salads, certain sauces, in mayonnaise and in garlic bread. Commercially it is used to flavour salts, and it is available in dehydrated flakes, or as a powder.

Medicinal

Garlic has remarkable medicinal properties, and is known, because of its penetrating quality, to be a natural and powerful antiseptic. It contains the vitamins A, B, and C, as well as

As well as imparting its unique flavour to a great many dishes, garlic is said to aid digestion.

copper, sulphur, manganese, iron and calcium, which make it valuable as a tonic for the cells and glands. People were bidden to eat it to cleanse the intestines, to help lower high blood-pressure, to expel worms, to ward off colds, to ease chest congestion and to alleviate rheumatism, while the raw juice was put on sterilized swabs during World War I and applied to wounds to prevent them turning septic. Garlic taken in capsule form is recommended when travelling overseas to help avoid infection. It is said to be beneficial to elderly people suffering from hardening of the arteries and general ageing symptoms, while many people with sinus trouble and hay-fever have been helped by taking garlic regularly.

Cosmetic

Garlic's contribution to cosmetic care is the work it does on the inside, as it has a remarkable effect on clearing the complexion. If the taking of garlic — either in capsule form or eating the raw cloves — is perservered with for a few days, a pimply skin will become quite clear and unblemished.

Companion planting

Garlic and roses benefit each other in the garden, garlic helping to repel aphids. But garlic near peas and beans will inhibit their growth. Pieces of garlic put amongst grain is an old European method of protecting it against weevils. A garden spray made from freshly crushed garlic cloves is a natural deterrent against many pests, and there are now garlic sprays already made up, which are available in specialty garden shops.

HORSERADISH

(Cochlearis armoracia) Cruciferae.
  Perennial.

Propagation: *root cuttings. Spring.*
Position: *shady.*
Soil: *rich, loose, moist.*
Height: *90 cm (3 feet).*
Part used: *root.*

Description

Horseradish has large, dark-green leaves resembling spinach, which under ideal conditions can grow up to 60 cm (2 feet) long. Being soft and fleshy, they are constantly attacked by leaf-eating pests, especially snails. The root system comprises a main or tap root about 30 cm (12 inches) long and 12 mm (½ inch) thick, with several smaller roots branching out from it at different angles. It is white in colour and rather like a radish, but is more hairy and wrinkled.

History and mythology

Like all herbs, horseradish has been known and valued by various groups of the human race through the ages, while today it has a wide and faithful following in different countries. It is thought to have originated in Eastern Europe and has become part of the diet of many people. It was a favourite condiment with vinegar amongst the hard-working country folk in rustic Germany. Its reputation spread to England and France, where it became known as *Moutarde des Allemands*. It is a member of the same family as mustard and cress and is rich in sulphur.

Cultivation

When planting, select the area required according to the number of plants you wish to grow, allowing 30 cm (12 inches) between plants each way. For instance, if wishing to grow four plants, the area needed will be 60 square cm (2 square feet). Measure out a plot of ground this size and dig a hole about 45 cm (1½ feet) deep, spreading some well decayed manure in the bottom before replacing the loose well broken soil back in the hole. Do this in winter, about one month before planting. In early spring, after selecting four straight main roots 20 cm (8 inches) long, cut off any side roots and plant them in the prepared bed, making a hole 30 cm (12 inches) long and 25 mm (1 inch) wide for each root and pour a little sand around the sides before covering with soil. Keep plants watered so that the roots do not become coarse.

Harvesting and processing

When the roots are cut for use, soil is scraped away from the side of the plant, and with a knife the small roots are then cut away from the main one, the small roots being the ones used. This can be done at any time. Every two years it is advisable to pull the whole plant out, keeping the long main roots for replanting. The side roots can be stored for some time in dry sand.

Various uses

Culinary

If you cannot grow your own horseradish, dried horseradish root which has been commercially prepared in the form of small grains or flakes, is now available. These swell and reconstitute in liquid, giving a good texture. Powdered horseradish root is not recommended as it is weaker in flavour and has no texture. A little freshly grated or dried horseradish in spreads, dressings and sauces gives an interesting tang. Horseradish sauce makes a tasty accompaniment to roast, grilled or boiled beef, pork, fish and poultry. Freshly grated apple mixes well with horseradish when making sauce, as does chopped mint. A little freshly grated or dried horseradish is excellent in a traditional bread sauce.

Medicinal

Anyone who enjoys the biting taste of grated horseradish will be interested to know that it also has a number of beneficial properties. It has long been known as a stimulant for many parts of the circulatory system, while having antiseptic qualities too. When taken with rich food it assists digestion, and when a little horseradish is grated into salads and taken regularly it will build up resistance to coughs and colds — and these are only some of its contributions to good health. Another therapeutic quality, when it is taken in a more con-

Horseradish has dark green leaves which can grow to 60 cm long under good conditions. But it is the root of this herb which is most widely used in cooking.

centrated form, is its ability to reduce catarrhal and bronchial complaints if one has succumbed to these ailments. (Once when suffering from a chest cold, I had a treatment of a horseradish and avocado rub, finished off under a hot lamp for fifteen minutes. It was very effective). Horseradish taken inwardly also relieves sinus pain and is said to help reduce blood pressure. An old recipe in a book of ours under the heading "To Relieve a Heavy Cold" says: "Grate horseradish, and inhale the fumes that arise."

Cosmetic

Some beauty herbalists use horseradish root in conjunction with other herbs to relieve eczema. It is also used with yoghurt or milk to be dabbed on the skin to fade freckles. For an effective skin-refresher, infuse some of the sliced root in milk and pat the milk on the skin.

Companion planting

Horseradish aids fruit trees in the orchard and helps prevent brown rot on apple trees. In the vegetable garden, horseradish, if kept restricted to the corners of the potato bed will assist potatoes to be more healthy and resistant to disease.

LAVENDER

Labitae. Perennial.

Lavender, English: *(Lavanduala spica, or L. officianalis, or L. vera).*
Lavender, French: *(L. dentata).*
Lavender, Italian or Spanish: *(L. stoechas).*
Propagation: *seeds, cuttings. Spring.*
Position: *sunny.*
Soil: *well drained.*
Height:
 English lavender 90 cm (3 feet).
 French lavender 1.5 m (5 feet).
 Italian lavender 60 cm (2 feet).
Part used: *leaves, flowers.*

Description

Among the various types of lavender, the most highly perfumed of plants, there are three basic kinds, known individually as English, French and Italian lavender. There are many hybridized versions, some of them quite hardy and successful, like *L. allardii,* which is larger than most lavenders and has the long flower spikes and smooth leaves of English lavender, while the foliage has the indented edges of French lavender. There are several strains that have been developed from English lavender. Some are dwarf, others have blooms in colours of white, pink or deep purple.

English lavender seems to be everyone's favourite. It is a bushy, small shrub growing 90 cm (3 feet) high, with silvery, smooth, pointed leaves and highly perfumed, tiny, mauve flowers which grow at the end of long, spiky stems. When the bush starts blooming in summer it is a beautiful sight, especially if several plants are massed together as a hedge. This type of planting suits all the lavenders. English lavender is the most often used for making lavender articles and the highest concentration of essential oil is in the flowers.

French lavender is the hardiest, and in many ways the most rewarding of the varieties to grow. It can reach a height of 1.5 metres (5 feet). The bush blooms continuously for about nine months of the year, especially if

(Left) French lavender
(Centre) English lavender
(Right) Italian lavender

mature flower stalks are cut back regularly to where two new shoots are beginning to branch. This helps to keep the bush a good shape while preventing it from having to feed flowers which are past their peak. These blooms can be dried for pot-pourri and sweet bags. Their perfume, although excellent, is not as potent as that of English lavender. The blooms are pale mauve and grow in a close head at the tip of a long, square stalk. If the location of the plant is particularly sunny, there will be a greater depth of colour in the flowers. French lavender heads are very attractive bunched closely together for posies. The grey leaves are rough and serrated, densely covering the bush, giving it a thick, hazy look. Use them dried in mixtures for pot-pourri and sleep pillows.

Italian lavender is sometimes known as Spanish lavender, and occasionally, but wrongly,

Lavender has long been a favourite with home gardeners. This English strain has white flowers.

French lavender is also very popular, although its fragrance is not as potent as English lavender.

Perhaps the best-known of the English lavenders is this sweet-scented strain with its mauve flowers.

The flowers of the French lavender are very pretty when bunched together and are often used in pot pourri.

as French lavender. It is a scarcer variety than the others, but well worth cultivating. This type does not usually grow more than 60 cm (2 feet) high. Although similar to the other lavenders, it is also different enough to make a contrast in the garden. The grey leaves are tiny, smooth and pointed and grow abundantly all over the bush. We have a curved hedge of ten bushes growing together at the top of a low embankment, and from mid-winter through to early summer they are covered with deep purple flowers that look rather like smaller versions of French lavender flowers, except for a little top-knot of petal tufts at the end of each flower head. Blossoms and leaves of Italian lavender are not as highly perfumed as other lavenders, but the blooms make

attractive posies. It was sometimes known fondly as "sticadove".

History and mythology

All the lavenders are native to the Mediterranean regions; the variety we call English lavender was not cultivated in England until about 1568. It was a favourite with the ancient Greeks, and one herbal writer of old says that it was known by the name of *Nardus,* from *Naarda,* a Syrian city near the river Euphrates, and that it was this herb which St. Mark referred to as "spikenard" in the Bible. Shakespeare refers to it, calling it "hot lavender" in *The Winter's Tale.*

Cultivation

The three basic types of lavender can be propagated from seed. If a hybrid lavender sets seed which is then planted, the new plants will probably revert back to the original type, so these must be increased by taking cuttings. If starting from seed, do this in spring by sowing into shallow drills in prepared seed boxes. Tip cuttings of any variety are taken when the soft, new leaves are firm enough not to wilt when they are put into a pot of sand. This is usually in late spring. When the seedlings are big enough, or when the cuttings have made roots, plant them out in a sunny, well drained position. This is very important for lavender, as it will not grow sturdily, nor flower well, if planted in a shady or damp place. When lavenders are in a position they like, the difference in the size of the bushes and the depth of colour in the flowers is very marked.

Harvesting and processing

The best time to pick and dry English lavender is before the last flowers on each stalk are fully opened. This is when their oil content is highest. Harvest the stalks on a dry day before the heat of the sun has drawn out the volatile essence, then tie them in bunches and hang in a shady, airy place to dry. When ready, strip the flowers from the stems and store them in

Italian lavender, also known as Spanish lavender, is a scarcer variety which makes very attractive posies.

airtight containers. When the plants have finished flowering, prune them hard, but not to ground level!

Leafy and flowering stalks of French lavender may be cut at any time for drying, providing there is no moisture in the air and the harvesting is done before midday. Hang in bunches and dry like English lavender. Prune the bushes quite severely when they have finished flowering.

Various uses

Culinary

Lavender is not usually thought of as a culinary herb these days. Several centuries ago, many sweet-scented flowers were employed in the kitchen quite extensively, and there is a recipe by "W. M. Cook to Queen Henrietta Maria, 1655" for a conserve of lavender flowers, which consists of lavender petals finely chopped, then mixed with icing sugar and enough rosewater to make a thin paste to spread as a fragrant icing on plain cakes and biscuits. Lavender vinegar for salads has a pleasant delicate flavour, and is made by in-

Although Italian lavender is smaller, only growing to a height of about 60 cm, its smooth grey leaves and deep purple flowers make a pleasant contrast in the garden when grown with other lavenders.

fusing whole lavender stalks, with their flowers, in white vinegar for several weeks.

Medicinal

The piercing, exquisite perfume of lavender flowers has a similar reviving effect as smelling salts when inhaled, for it is known that lavender calms the nerves and relaxes tensions. A bath at night impregnated with a few drops of lavender oil soothes and relaxes the peripheral nerves, while lavender flowers in a sedative tea mixture will help to bring on sleep. The leaves, as well as the flowers, have this wondrous effect. Notice the next time you are stripping a quantity of dried lavender how drowsy you will become. Besides this, lavender was recognized as having a good effect on the digestion. Lavender essence has been widely used as a remedy for giddiness and faintness, nervous palpitations and flatulence. It was administered by putting a few drops on sugar or in a little milk. Oil of lavender is still used by modern herbalists to rub into rheumatic joints to ease pain. It is also claimed that rubbing oil of lavender on burns does not relieve the pain, but assists with healing scar tissue.

Cosmetic

Lavender toilet water seems always to have been available. It is antiseptic for the skin, refreshing, and is especially recommended for an oily complexion and pimples. Fresh or dried lavender flowers or leaves tied in a muslin bag and infused in hot bath water give the skin an all-over fragrance (use oil of lavender instead if you wish). Who does not respond to the wholesome smell of lavender-perfumed sheets and pillow cases? Lavender perfumed note paper and cards were once very much in vogue too. Lavender is indispensable in pot-pourri mixtures, in lavender filled coat hangers, in lavender bags and for making lavender "bottles". Because of its soothing qualities, lavender is essential inside "sleep pillows". The warmth of the head releases the perfume and induces tranquil slumber. Not only the flowers are used, but the leaves as well. Never throw away the foliage, besides being perfumed, it provides valuable bulk when needed.

Companion planting

Lavender associates well with thyme in the garden. As a highly aromatic herb it has a good influence on vegetables growing nearby, helping to make healthier plants with more flavour. When in bloom, lavender attracts myriads of honey bees and butterflies of all colours. Lavender also helps repel moths and other undesirable insects, in clothes cupboards and in carpets.

61

LOVAGE

(Levisicum officinale) Umbelliferae.
Perennial.

Propagation: *seeds. Spring.*
Position: *semi-shade.*
Soil: *rich, moist.*
Height: *90 cm-1.50 m (3-5 feet).*
Part used: *root, stems, leaves, seeds.*

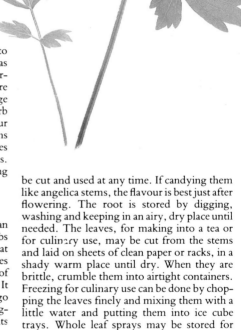

Description

In appearance, lovage bears a resemblance to
angelica, although it does not grow as tall or as
densely. The flowers are smaller and sulphur-
yellow, while angelica's great round heads are
white to lime-green. When young, lovage
plants also look like a rather obscure herb
called smallage said to be the forerunner of our
modern celery. Lovage's slim, hollow stems
bear flat, serrated, dark green leaves in threes
branching out from thicker, channeled stalks.
The yellow flowers are followed by oblong
brown seeds.

History and mythology

Lovage originated from the Mediterranean
region and is one of the lesser known herbs
today, yet it was formerly employed a great
deal in medicine and cooking. In ancient times
it grew wild in the mountainous districts of
northern Greece and the south of France. It
found its way to Britain many centuries ago
and became one of the most cultivated of English herbs for use in herbal medicine for its
root, stems, leaves and seeds.

Cultivation

Like angelica, lovage likes rich, moist soil and
a rather shady position to grow well. The seed
can be sown in prepared boxes, or in the open
ground in spring. When seedlings are about
8 cm (3 inches) high, plant them out to 45 cm
(1½ feet) apart. Keep them watered in dry
weather.

Harvesting and processing

Harvest the seed just before it starts to fall by
snipping off and drying whole flower-heads.
Sift out any dried husks and stalks and store
the seed in airtight containers. The stems can

be cut and used at any time. If candying them
like angelica stems, the flavour is best just after
flowering. The root is stored by digging,
washing and keeping in an airy, dry place until
needed. The leaves, for making into a tea or
for culinary use, may be cut from the stems
and laid on sheets of clean paper or racks, in a
shady warm place until dry. When they are
brittle, crumble them into airtight containers.
Freezing for culinary use can be done by chop-
ping the leaves finely and mixing them with a
little water and putting them into ice cube
trays. Whole leaf sprays may be stored for
several weeks in the freezer when sealed in
foil.

Various uses

Culinary

The flavour of the leaves resembles a combination of celery and parsley, but predomi-
nantly celery, with an extra peppery bite.
They make an excellent, healthful addition to
salads, soups, stews and some sauces. For
those on a condiment-free diet, use lovage for
its spicy peppery taste. Chop the leaves finely
for best results, as they are a little coarse. The
hollow stalks and stems are often preserved as
a confection in the same way as angelica.

Lovage flourishes in a rich, moist soil and is best grown in a sheltered position. Today it is not one of the better known herbs, but in the past it was used extensively in both cooking and medicine. The leaves have a peppery tang which adds zest to soups, stews, salads and sauces.

Medicinal

The roots, stems, leaves and seeds of lovage were used in herbal medicine for stomach disorders and feverish attacks. An infusion of the root was considered beneficial in many illnesses, including jaundice and urinary troubles. A decoction of the seeds was recommended as a gargle for infections of the mouth and throat, as a drink for pleurisy and as a lotion for bathing sore eyes. The leaves eaten raw in a salad, or infused dry as a tea, are still recognized as being stimulating for the digestive organs and helpful in remedying gynaecological disturbances. In special diets, the chopped leaves are an excellent substitute for pepper and other hot spices. Lovage was also regarded as an important pot herb in days gone by. In some regions where fresh vege-

tables are scarce, the roots are used for food and it is believed that chewing the stems will help prevent infection.

Cosmetic

Lovage is considered to be a deodorising herb, both in solutions for the outside of the body, and as an inner cleanser for the system so as to acquire a clear skin outwardly. After a strenuous day, when one has perspired freely, try a lovage bath as an all-over body freshener. Make a strong tea with the leaves and add to a hot bath, or pick fresh leaves, bruise them and put them straight into the bath water. This is a very old custom going back beyond the Middle Ages.

Companion planting

Lovage, as an aromatic herb, has a generally beneficial effect in the garden when sown in small patches, or as a border. Aromatic herbs have a particularly enlivening effect on the more stolid vegetable plants such as potatoes, swedes and other root vegetables.

MARJORAM & OREGANO

Marjoram: *(Origanum majorana)*
  Labiatae. Perennial.
Oregano: *(O. vulgare) Labiatae.*
  Perennial.
Propagation: *seeds, cuttings. Spring.*
Position: *sunny.*
Soil: *average, well-drained.*
Height: *marjoram 45 cm (1½ feet).*
    oregano 60 cm (2 feet).
Part used: *leaves.*

Description

These two herbs are so closely related and
their cultivation is so similar, that it is not
necessary to classify them in separate sections.
However, in appearance they are slightly different. Marjoram leaves are small, soft and a
grey-green colour, while oregano leaves are
light green and are much firmer. Their growing habit is also different. Marjoram is a
compact, upright, shrubby plant while oregano has a dense, spreading habit. The flowers
of both these herbs are small and white and
form tight clusters at the tips of their stems.
The herb we know as oregano is a wild form
of marjoram. It is more robust, coarser in
texture and stronger in flavour than its gentler
cousin, the sweet marjoram of our herb
gardens. There are variations of both oregano
and marjoram, which are all easy to identify as
their scent and leaf texture are characteristic of
each strain. Oregano is always more piercing
in scent, although the leaves of other forms
may vary in size and the flowers in colour. The
marjoram described here has white, tufted

flowers on long stems. There is another quite common kind known as knotted marjoram with tiny, white flowers bursting out from tight green "knots". The aromas are the same.

The marjoram plant is just coming into flower. When the blooms appear, they are in tight clusters. The flower heads together with the leaves are used in cooking.

History and mythology

Botanically, these herbs are all *origanums*. Scholars tell us they first grew in the Mediterranean regions and were also widely distributed in parts of Asia and North Africa. Marjoram was one of the strewing herbs once used to give houses a pleasant, clean smell and it was a favourite in sweet bags for the linen cupboard. John Gerard, the sixteenth century herbalist, mentions it as "marvellous sweet" and "aromaticall". Another old herbalist says that to smell marjoram frequently keeps a person in good health.

Cultivation

To propagate these plants by cuttings, take new shoots about 8 cm (3 inches) long in late spring, when the young leaves have firmed enough not to wilt when placed in a pot of coarse river sand. When well rooted, they can be planted out in pots, or put straight into the ground, leaving at least 30 cm (12 inches) between them. When growing from seeds, sow them in a prepared seed-box in spring and plant them out when the seedlings are 8 cm

(3 inches) high. Both have a tendency to become woody as they get older, so to delay this as long as possible, it is advisable to cut out the old wood at the end of winter before the new spring growth appears. After approximately four years, the plants often become so woody that it is best to replace them.

Harvesting and processing

Both marjoram and oregano should be harvested just before the plants are in full flower in the summer or early autumn. Cut the long stems, together with any flower-heads, and hang them in bunches in a cool, airy place. The leaves tend to fall as they dry, so it is a good idea to enclose the bunches in mosquito net or muslin. When the leaves and flowers are crisp-dry they are very easily stripped by running the thumb and forefinger down the stems. When stored in airtight containers they will stay fresh for many months, and for pungency and flavour they will be almost equal, and sometimes better, than the fresh leaves. For freezing, chop fresh leaves finely, mix them with a little water and put them into ice

cube trays in the freezer. Sprays of fresh marjoram or oregano may be wrapped in foil, sealed and kept in the deep freeze for some weeks. Marjoram or oregano butter may also be frozen. Chop the fresh leaves, pound them into softened butter, allow it to set in the refrigerator, then cut it into squares and seal into small polythene bags or other suitable containers.

Various uses

Culinary

The Greeks call wild marjoram or oregano, *rigani*, and in Greece, as in Italy, it is the very pungent dried flower-tops which are mainly used in cooking. Marjoram of course, is a classic ingredient in traditional mixed herbs, together with thyme and sage. Marjoram's subtle aroma makes it an ideal addition to many herb mixtures as it helps give "body" and depth without being too dominant. On its own, it goes with poultry, fish, egg dishes, vegetable dishes and sauces. Put it into salads, scones, dumplings and clear soups.

Oregano's pungency is even stronger when dried and this herb is a popular ingredient in the tasty regional dishes of many countries. It is used in pasta and rice dishes, in pizzas, moussaka, avocado dip, tomato dishes, meat loaf, rissoles, sauces and dressings, and with zucchini, capsicums and eggplant. It is often sprinkled on beef, lamb and pork before cooking.

Oregano is closely related to marjoram, but has a coarser texture and a stronger flavour.

Medicinal

Greek physicians used marjoram or oregano extensively, both internally and externally. The cosmic warmth it has accumulated from the sun helps put right bad colds, cramps and digestive disorders. Hot fomentations of the dried leaves and tops applied in bags is helpful to painful swellings, rheumatism and colic. An infusion of the leaves taken as a tea relieves nervous headaches, induces sleep, stimulates excretion and is recommended as a spring tea.

Cosmetic

Marjoram, like sage, will help darken hair for brunettes, and for this purpose may be made into lotions or rubs for the head, or for a beard. Marjoram sprigs tied into a bath bag are refreshing. Dried marjoram leaves are a fragrant addition to a sleep pillow blend and to a pot-pourri mixture.

Companion planting

Marjoram and oregano, by their fragrant presence in the garden, are a good influence on other plants and when they are in flower they are a strong attraction to honey bees. It is said that marjoram has been fed to cows to prevent abortion. After calving, marjoram mixed with balm and made into a tea is given to cows to soothe and strengthen them. Marjoram's content of essential oil increases if stinging nettle is growing nearby as a companion plant.

MINT

(Mentha) labiatae. Perennial.

Applemint: *(M. rotundifolia)*.
Eau-de-Cologne Mint: *(M. piperita citrata)*.
Pennyroyal: *(M. pulegium)*.
Peppermint: *(M. piperita officinalis)*.
Spearmint: *(M. spicata, or M. crispa, or M. viridis)*.
Propagation: *cuttings, root division, seed. Spring.*
Position: *semi-shade to shade.*
Soil: *rich, moist.*
Height: *30-90 cm (1-3 feet) according to variety.*
Part used: *leaves.*

Eau-de-Cologne mint

Variegated applemint

Description

The mints are a versatile family; there are quite a number with pronouncedly different fla-vours and scents, even though between them there is a strong outward resemblance, except for leaf colour. We have listed five easily available varieties, although other more rare kinds include watermint, cornmint, catnip, Japanese peppermint, American wild mint. Egyptian mint, Corsican mint, woolly mint, European horse mint, liquorice mint, ginger mint, basil mint, lemon mint, and Asian mint (very hot). Mints hybridize with each other, which is one of the reasons for the wide diversity of types.

Applemint, as the name suggests, has a strong scent of apples. Growing approxi-mately 30 cm (12 inches) high, it has oval, wrinkled, soft leaves and small white flowers which appear in autumn. Sometimes this variety is called *pineapple mint*. Another vari-ation is *variegated applemint,* also sometimes called *golden applemint* and *variegated lemon balm.* The reason for the different common name for the same plant comes about through mistaken identification, and after some time the incorrect name sticks.

Eau-de-Cologne mint is yet another variety with several names. We have seen it listed both as bergamot mint and orange mint. This type has smooth, green leaves tinged with purple; they are oval in shape and grow up to 8 cm

Lemon mint

Basil mint

Lemon mint in flower

Asian mint

Pennyroyal

*Crinkle-leaved
spearmint*

Peppermint

Smooth-leaved spearmint

(3 inches) long and 25 mm (1 inch) across, with a strong, sharp perfume. The stems are square (as with all mints) and purple in colour. The plants may reach a height of 90 cm (3 feet). In autumn it bears flowers typical of all mints, except that these are larger and a deep shade of mauve, making them a pretty addition to mixed posies.

Pennyroyal is another member of the mint family. It has small, shiny green leaves and a strong peppermint scent. It has a creeping habit and for most of the year never grows higher than 25 mm (1 inch) above the ground. For this reason it makes a good ground cover in a shady part of the garden. In spring the mauve flowers appear in a series of circlets along 30 cm (12 inches) high stems. When flowering has finished, plants can be cut down with the mower, thus making a lawn that needs no other attention, except for watering in dry weather.

Peppermint is a most useful plant as it is the herb that yields the true oil of peppermint. Growing to about 60 cm (2 feet) high, it has small, pointed, green leaves with a purple tint. The scent is so characteristically peppermint that it cannot be mistaken for any other mint.

Spearmint can have either elongated, smooth, bright green leaves, or oval-shaped, crinkly, dark green leaves, according to the variety. Both varieties have the same vital, typical mint scent. The smooth-leaved variety is often called English spearmint and is more difficult to grow than its coarser brother. The scent and flavour is clearer and stronger and the leaves have a finer texture, but it is susceptible to diseases and leaf-eating insects. Either of these mints is the most suitable for culinary purposes, and can be grown in the garden in a moist position, or in a large tub under a dripping tap.

History and mythology

Mint's history goes back to Greek mythology and to Biblical times. The Romans introduced it to Britain and it was familiar to Chaucer and Shakespeare. One Greek historian wrote that: "The smell of Mint does stir up the minde and the taste to a greedy desire of meate." The Pharisees in the Bible were paid tithes of mint, anise and cumin. Chaucer writes of "a little path of mintes full and fenill greene."

Cultivation

Mints are usually propagated by root division, as even the smallest piece will grow. How-

Pennyroyal has a matting, creeping habit and for this reason it makes an excellent groundcover.

A bed of peppermint has a very characteristic smell and from this herb peppermint oil is obtained.

Eau-de-Cologne mint has smooth green leaves with a purple tinge and an attractive mauve flower.

Crinkly-leaved spearmint is one of two varieties, the other having elongated, smooth leaves.

ever, if this is not possible, short stem cuttings taken after the new growth has hardened in late spring can be put straight into the ground, where roots will quickly form. They are best grown in rich, moist soil, in semi-shade, but will also grow in poor, sandy soil if the ground is fertilized from time to time. Cut the plants back to ground level in winter. If mint is attacked by rust, the plants must be dug out and burnt, starting again with new stock in a different part of the garden. Mint is not usually propagated by seed because it is small and difficult to harvest. If however, you grow mint from seed, sow in spring in prepared seed boxes, keep moist, and when the plants are large enough to handle, plant them out.

Harvesting and processing

Mints will dry satisfactorily by hanging the leafy stems, cut just before coming into full flower, in bunches in a dry, airy place. Make sure that when the crisp, dried leaves are stripped from their stalks they are kept in airtight containers, as this herb does not keep its full aroma and flavour if exposed to the air for long. For freezing, chop fresh leaves finely, mix them with a little water and put them into ice cube trays in the freezer. Sprays of fresh mint may be wrapped in foil, sealed and kept in the deep freeze for some weeks. Spearmint butter may also be frozen and is delicious with lamb. Chop the fresh leaves, pound them into softened butter, allow to set in the refrigerator, then cut into squares and seal into small polythene bags or other suitable containers. Small sprigs of peppermint or eau-de-Cologne mint may be individually frozen in ice cube trays in the summer, then dropped into cooling beverages on hot days.

Various uses

Culinary

Applemint can be mixed with spearmint for mint sauce. When frying bananas for chicken Maryland, roll them first in finely chopped applemint. Mix the chopped leaves into fruit salads and fruit jellies. Be adventurous and try new flavour combinations with this fresh-tasting herb.

Eau-de-Cologne mint has a flavour too powerful to use in any quantity, although one chopped leaf added to a mixture of other herbs gives a delicious tang. A bunch of this mint in a jug of water on a hot day seems to help cool the surrounding atmosphere.

Pennyroyal is not recommended for culinary use as it brings on abortions in cattle, and is said to do the same thing with human beings! If you are not at risk, we have found a few chopped leaves with new potatoes and butter very pleasant.

Spearmint either fresh or dried, is the variety which gives mint sauce its flavour, as well as being used in mint jelly and mint julep. It is customary with green peas. Chopped mint goes with hot, buttered new potatoes, with tomatoes, in some egg dishes, in custards and ice cream. A few fresh leaves on buttered bread with cream cheese make delicious sandwiches.

Medicinal

A tea made from fresh or dried peppermint leaves not only tastes pleasant, but if one is suffering from a heavy cold or indigestion, some relief comes soon after one or two cups. This beverage is also a soothing, relaxing drink, helping to promote sound, natural sleep, especially appreciated by students whose minds may be over-active through prolonged study. It is said that if peppermint tea is taken regularly in autumn and then all through the winter, it helps build up a resistance to colds. As a routine, either start the day with a cup, or have it before going to bed at night. In summer, iced peppermint tea is refreshing, and a quantity can be made and kept in the refrigerator for one or two days.

Spearmint tea is revivifying too. A friend found that drinking spearmint tea while she was staying in Singapore for some time was most satisfying and refreshing. Peppermint and spearmint tea are becoming much more available now and are often sold in tea bags. They are also excellent when blended with other teas to make them more palatable. Children generally will like peppermint or spearmint tea.

Cosmetic

Spearmint will help to prevent bad breath, and is incorporated into a number of herbal toothpastes for this reason. It also helps to whiten teeth and condition the gums. Spearmint has a beneficial effect on the head, and was used to wash children's heads when inclined to sores. Both spearmint and peppermint are excellent for conditioning oily hair. Oil of spearmint (mint) in the bath is stimulating and even float-

ing a few sprigs of fresh mint in hot bath water is effective. Spearmint has also been used for helping heal chapped hands. Dried eau-de-Cologne mint leaves make an excellent fragrant addition to pot-pourri and sleep pillows.

Companion planting

Peppermint in the vegetable garden aids cabbage plants. It has been found that the oil is greatly increased in peppermint plants if they are grown with stinging nettles. It has also been noted that production of the oil is retarded in peppermint plants if they are grown with chamomile, but that the chamomile itself will have a greater oil content.

Spearmint is an excellent insect repellent and will help to keep away black flea beetles, cabbage, butterfly caterpillars, ants, fleas and, to a certain extent, aphis. Spearmint is reported to repel various rodents. Indoors, dried mint leaves placed in drawers and cupboards keep away moths. Mint was valued as a strewing herb in houses, both for its perfume and insect repellent qualities. All varieties have the reputation for preventing milk from curdli..g. Sprigs of mint placed in a room will overcome the smell of stale tabacco.

Pennyroyal when growing wild in pastures brings on abortions in cows. It is an excellent flea and mosquito repellent. It also repels ants. If sitting outside, or working in the garden, fresh pennyroyal rubbed on the skin is a protection against mosquitoes.

Both varieties of spearmint are widely used in the kitchen, either fresh or dried. They give their flavour to mint sauce, mint jelly and julep and are a delicious accompaniment to green peas.

PARSLEY

Parsley, Curled *(Petroselinum crispum) Umbelliferae. Biennial.*
Parsley, Italian: *(P. crispum neapolitanum) Umbelliferae. Biennial.*
Propagation: *seeds. Spring (again in Autumn in temperate climates).*
Position: *sunny.*
Soil: *average, well drained.*
Height: *curled parsley, 25 cm (10 inches) Italian parsley, 45 cm (1½ feet).*
Part used: *leaves, root (sometimes).*

Description

Curled parsley, as the name suggests, has tightly curled leaves of bright green. Some kinds may be more crinkled and tightly curled than others, for instance the triple-curled and moss-curled varieties. *P. crispum* is the variety of curled parsley that people usually refer to as parsley, and is the most widely used.

Italian parsley, which is not so familiar, has leaves which are not curled, but are deeply cut and serrated like the tops of celery or lovage, the flavour being regarded by many as stronger than curled parsley. However, curled parsley is preferred for garnishing because of its more decorative leaves. There is another variety called Hamburg parsley which has a long, white root like a parsnip and is mainly grown for these roots which can be cooked and eaten as a vegetable.

History and mythology

It is widely believed that parsley originated in Sardinia, although an early writer says that parsley has the "curious botanic history that no one can tell what is its native country. Probably the plant has been so altered by cultivation as to have lost all likeness to its original self." It occurs in mythology, and was believed to have sprung from the blood of a Greek hero, Archemorous, the forerunner of death. The Greeks crowned the winners at the Isthmian games with parsley chaplets and warriors fed their chariot horses with the leaves. Grecian gardens were often bordered with parsley.

(Left) Curled parsley
(Right) Italian parsley

Cultivation

To propagate parsley, sow seed in spring and also in autumn in temperate climates, in finely dug soil, in drills 30 cm (12 inches) apart, where the plants are to grow, thinning out later to approximately 8 cm (3 inches) between plants. Curled parsley is the most difficult type to grow, the seeds sometimes taking two weeks to germinate, during which time the bed *must never* be allowed to dry out, or the seeds will cease germinating. If this has occurred, further watering is of no use, the seeds must be resown and more care taken. Covering them with up to 12 mm (½ inch) of soil will help retain moisture in the ground for a longer period. Italian parsley is much easier to grow. Three to four days after sowing, the seeds will usually germinate, provided that they are very lightly covered with soil to not more than 6 mm (¼ inch) in depth, and kept moist. As parsley is a biennial, to keep it from going to seed during the first year, cut the long flower-stalks as they appear. However, the second year's growth is never as good. We prefer to sow seed each year to ensure strong and healthy plants.

Harvesting and processing

Parsley can be cut for drying at any time. It will keep its green colour and flavour if dried quickly in a warm oven preheated to 120°C (250°F). After turning the oven off, spread out the parsley heads, which have been snipped from the stalks, on a large tray or baking dish, and leave in the oven for fifteen minutes, turning several times until crisp–dry. Store them in airtight containers away from the light. For freezing, chop fresh leaves finely, mix with a little water and put them into ice cube trays in the freezer. Sprays of fresh parsley may be wrapped in foil and frozen. Parsley butter freezes well too.

Various uses

Culinary

Parsley's taste could be described as fresh and crisp and perhaps a little earthy. It is also unassertive which makes it complimentary to other herbs in mixtures. For instance it is one

Although parsley is mainly thought of as an eating herb, it is most decorative when growing in the garden.

Parsley is such a versatile herb that no kitchen garden is complete without it. Lack of space is no problem as it can successfully be grown in tubs.

of four in a "fines herbes" blend, the others being chervil, chives and tarragon. A spray of

A stone trough (top) or this unusual Apostle jar look most attractive when used as a container for parsley grown by itself or with other herbs.

Medicinal

All parts of the plant, roots, stems, leaves and seeds, are useful and beneficial. The roots were once boiled and eaten as a vegetable, particularly the large Hamburg variety. The stalks of Italian parsley have been blanched and eaten like celery. The foliage of all varieties is rich in iron and in vitamins including A, B and C, and the culinary value is well known. An oil called apiol which is extracted from the seeds, has medicinal properties. Although nowadays the seeds are not normally used for culinary purposes, there is a story that the ninth century Emperor, Charlemagne, after having tasted a cheese flavoured with parsley seeds, ordered two cases of these cheeses to be sent to him yearly. Parsley tea made from leaves or root assists kidneys, digestion and circulation.

Cosmetic

Parsley has been included in rubbing lotions for the scalp and hair before shampooing, and to make dark hair shiny. Parsley is also used in herbal lotions for closing large pores and as a freshener for the skin and to reduce puffiness around the eyes.

Companion planting

Parsley is helpful to roses in the garden, a low border of curly parsley plants being attractive and beneficial at the same time. Parsley also aids tomatoes. Honey bees are attracted to parsley when it is in bloom.

parsley, together with a bay leaf and a spray each of thyme and marjoram, comprises a bouquet garni. Parsley leaves, whether freshly chopped or dried, go into sauces, omelettes, scrambled eggs, mashed potatoes, mornays, salads, soups, pasta dishes and vegetable dishes and with poultry and fish. The fresh curly sprays are used for garnishing and when crisp-fried make a delicious accompaniment for fish. Nourishing parsley jelly is made from the fresh leaves. Parsley tea is made from either the fresh or dried leaves.

ROSEMARY

Rosemary, Upright: *(Rosmarinus officinalis) Labiatae. Perennial.*

Rosemary, Prostrate: *(R. prostratus) Labiatae. Perennial.*

Propagation: *seeds, cuttings. Spring (Autumn in mild climates). Layering also for Prostrate Rosemary.*

Position: *open, sunny*

Soil: *average, well drained.*

Height: *Upright Rosemary 1.50m (5 feet) Prostrate Rosemary 30 cm (12 inches).*

Part used: *leaves.*

(Top) Upright rosemary
(Bottom) Prostrate rosemary

Description

The blossoms and leaves of these two rosemarys are similar in appearance. Both have the same kind of delicate-blue flowers and long, narrow leaves which are dark green on top and silver-striped underneath. The leaves of upright rosemary grow to over 25 mm (1 inch) long, while those of the low-growing or prostrate rosemary are smaller and narrower. There are several other unusual kinds of rosemary which are not often seen, including a white flowering variety, one with gold-edged leaves, and a double flowering type. The growth habit of the two rosemarys mentioned here is entirely different. Upright rosemary has a stiff, bushy habit, making it an ideal subject for hedge-work, while prostrate rosemary is grown more for ornamental purposes, as a ground cover, or to hang decoratively over the edge of retaining walls. It is excellent in rockeries and also in tubs, where it will spill towards the ground in a most attractive way. One landscape gardener told us that she had planted a sweep of prostrate rosemary on a sloping bank leading down to a swimming pool, where the blue of the flowers and the blue water seemed to reflect one another. Both varieties start blooming in the autumn and continue on through the winter until spring.

History and mythology

Rosemary is another aromatic plant which first grew in the warm countries of the Mediterranean region and it seems to be the upright variety which is referred to histori-cally. It has great beneficial properties which are still highly respected today. Of the many legends about rosemary, there is a popular one telling how a rosemary bush will never grow taller than the height of Christ 1.5 to 2 metres (5 to 6 feet) when He was a man on earth, and that after thirty-three years the plant increases in breadth, but not in height. Some stories tell how rosemary was used to try to awaken the Sleeping Beauty. The Sicilians tell their children that young fairies taking the form of snakes lie amongst the branches of rosemary bushes.

Cultivation

To propagate upright rosemary, sow the seed in spring, or in autumn where the climate is mild, in a prepared seed box. Plant out when the seedlings are 8 cm (3 inches) high, leaving about 60 cm (2 feet) between plants. Fifteen cm (6 inches) long tip cuttings may also be taken in late spring, when the soft spring

Because of its wiry, bushy growth habit, upright rosemary is very suitable for growing as a hedge.

Prostrate rosemary has a delicate trailing habit and looks most graceful when grown over a wall.

growth has hardened. The prostrate variety can only be satisfactorily propagated by taking cuttings, using the same method as for upright rosemary, or by layering, which is done by pinning down a stem from the parent plant to the soil, using a piece of U-shaped wire and covering the stem with a little soil. When the layered branch has developed a good root system, cut it away from the parent bush and plant out in a sunny position.

Harvesting and processing

Rosemary can be used fresh at any time, the upright variety being the most suitable for culinary purposes as the flavour is better. For drying, cut the branches before the plant begins flowering (when the flavour is at its best), shaping the bush at the same time. Then hang in bunches in a shady, airy place. When dry, strip the leaves from the stalks, crumbling them into small pieces. When stored in airtight containers, the flavour will remain intact over a long period. For freezing, strip the leaves carefully from their woody stalks and chop finely. Mix with a little water and put them into ice cube trays in the freezer. Sprays of fresh rosemary may be wrapped in foil, sealed and kept in the deep freeze for some weeks. Rosemary butter may also be frozen. Chop the fresh leaves, incorporate them into softened butter, allow to set in the refrigerator, then cut into squares and seal into small polythene bags or other suitable containers.

Various uses

Culinary

Rosemary is one of the most strongly pungent plants; the taste and scent of the crushed leaves are warmly vital, yet freshly resinous as well. This herb helps the digestion of rich and starchy food. It gives a delicious, savoury tang to beef, lamb, veal, pork, rabbit, goose, duck, and sometimes chicken, if it is a highly seasoned dish. Rosemary is used in liver pâté, and in spiced sauces for pasta. It goes well with eggplant, zucchini, lima beans, Brussels sprouts and cabbage. It is excellent in herb bread and in scones. Try stirring a tablespoon of the finely chopped leaves into your usual plain scone mixture before adding the liquid. The flavour is subtle and piquant, and when freshly buttered and hot from the oven, every morsel quickly disappears. The flowers can be candied.

Medicinal

It was believed since the earliest times, that rosemary stimulated the memory. Students in ancient Greece entwined the green sprigs in their hair while studying for examinations. This is the origin of the saying "rosemary for remembrance". Herbalists today recommend rosemary tea to strengthen the memory for those who suffer from forgetfulness, and to relieve headaches. In herbal medicine it is used

The saying 'Rosemary for remembrance' dates back to Ancient Greece and herbalists still believe that drinking rosemary tea can aid a poor memory.

as a nerve tonic and also for the digestion. Rosemary is also reputed to strengthen sight, and there is an old saying that "it comforts the heart and quickens the spirit". Rosemary wine is a quietening cordial for the nerves and is stimulating for the kidneys.

Cosmetic

Rosemary's main attribute is its association with all functions of the head. Extract of rosemary in shampoos and hair tonics revitalizes the scalp, prevents dandruff and encourages new and healthy hair growth with a shining lustre. These occurrences have been experienced personally by ourselves and our family. A few sprays of rosemary, or oil of rosemary, in the morning bath makes a bracing start to the day. But do not use it in an evening bath before going to bed, substitute lavender for its sedative qualities. Oil of rosemary also goes into eau-de-Cologne and the leaves and flowers are a fragrant addition to pot-pourri.

Companion planting

Rosemary and sage are good companion plants, having a stimulating effect upon each other. Rosemary repels carrot fly. Like other aromatic herbs, rosemary is a good influence in the garden. It attracts honey bees when in flower. Honey made from rosemary is delectable, like eating nectar. In the house, dried sprays of rosemary help to repel moths in drawers and cupboards.

SAGE

(Salvia officinalis) Labiatae. Perennial.

Propagation: *seeds, cuttings. Spring
   (Autumn in mild climates).*
Position: *sunny, elevated.*
Soil: *light, well drained.*
Height: *90 cm (3 feet).*
Part used: *leaves.*

Description

A sage bush in the garden is a most attractive
sight as well as being very useful. The aromatic, silver-grey leaves are approximately
8 cm (3 inches) long and 12 mm (½ inch)
across. However, when they first appear they
are a pale green colour, then as the leaves
mature and harden they turn grey. Bees are
fond of the purple, lipped flowers which start
blooming on long stems in the autumn, and
sometimes in spring. It has been said that
when the flowers open, each one resembles a
tiny lion's mouth that drinks in the fire of the
sun, the plant's chemistry transforming it into
an aromatic volatile oil that courses through it.

History and Mythology

Sage originated from the northern shores of
the Mediterranean. It has been cultivated for
culinary and medicinal uses for hundreds of
years in England, France and Germany. In
later years it was taken to America, and later
still to Australia. The name of the genus is
derived from the Latin *salvere,* to be saved,
referring to the curative powers of the plant.
An old tradition was to plant rue amongst
valuable sage plants to keep away noxious
toads. Sage was also believed to assuage grief,
and in Pepys' Diary he notes the planting of
sage on graves in a country churchyard. One
of its earliest reputations was as a preventative
against the onslaughts of old age: "He who
would live for aye must eat sage in May" is an
old English proverb. The ancient Egyptians
used sage medicinally as a brain tonic. The
Chinese valued it for the same reason,

Cultivation

To propagate from seed, sow in spring (in
mild climates autumn sowing is also possible

in a prepared seed box). When seedlings have
reached a height of 10 cm (4 inches) plant them
out, leaving 60 cm (2 feet) between each one in
a well drained and sunny position that is also
elevated if possible. Water the plants well
while they are young. When sage becomes an
established plant, water only in dry weather as
it will not thrive if conditions are too damp. It
is most noticeable that plants with grey leaves
do not usually like wet feet or moist conditions. When propagating from cuttings, use
15 cm (6 inch) long, new shoots after the leaves
have hardened and become grey; this happens
in late spring, or possibly earlier, according to
the season. Plant out when cuttings have
developed roots.

Harvesting and Processing

Harvest sage for drying just before the plant
flowers. A successful method is to hang loosely
bundled long sprays tied together in a cool,
airy place. The branches may also be laid out
on racks to dry in a warm position, but never
in direct sunlight. When dry and brittle, pull
off all the leaves and store in airtight containers
immediately, as it is unwise to leave the bun-
dles, attractive though they are, to gather
dust. By the way, it is important when cutting

Established sage does not need much watering.

Sage is a most attractive herb to grow in the garden, with its silver-grey leaves and purple-lipped flowers that bloom in autumn and sometimes in spring.

These sage seedlings have reached a height of 10 cm and are ready for transplanting into pots.

sage at any time, to prune out any dead twigs and branches, as the plant can become very woody as it grows older. Fresh sage leaves may also be chopped finely, put into ice cube trays, covered with water and allowed to freeze. It will keep for many months like this. When needed, either drop a sage cube into the food you are cooking, or allow to thaw and then use.

Various uses

Culinary

Sage leaves whether fresh or dry, counteract the richness in certain foods while assisting the digestion. Use sage on its own, or with other herbs, when cooking pork; goose, duck, veal and oily fish. It goes into pea soup, bean soup, and vegetable soup. Cook sage with onions, eggplant, tomatoes, cheese dishes, egg dishes, rich cream sauces, breads, dumplings and scones. Sage is a necessary ingredient in mixed herbs, along with thyme and marjoram.

Medicinal

Sage is believed to restore energy and bad memory, and is known to be helpful to the digestion, having a tonic effect on the liver. Sage tea is still taken today as a nerve tonic, and is recommended as a regular beverage for people who are studying for examinations and need to rely on their memory. This herb has also long been known to be beneficial for the mouth and throat, and is still included by some manufacturers in mouth washes and gargles. In olden days the leaves have been used for tobacco, for tea, in cheeses and breads. Because of its antiseptic properties it was used as a strewing herb on floors to keep away unwanted insects and vermin.

Cosmetic

Sage is still used in some commercial hair tonics to prevent hair from going grey. A simple old method for whitening teeth was to rub a fresh sage leaf over them each day. Sage is also used in recipes for cleansing lotions for the skin, in deodorants, hair rinses, and for large pores, in setting lotions and in neck creams.

Companion Planting

In the garden, sage and rosemary aid one another. Sage also helps to repel cabbage butterfly and improve the flavour and digestibility of cabbages if grown amongst them.

SALAD BURNET

(Sanguisorba minor) Rosaceae.
Perennial.

Propagation: *seed. Spring (again in*
Autumn in temperate climates).
Position: *sunny.*
Soil: *average.*
Height: *30 cm (12 inches).*
Part used: *leaves.*

Description

This herb has cucumber-flavoured leaves that
are small, round and serrated. They are spaced
about 25 mm (1 inch) apart in pairs of ten or
twelve on each side of a slender stem. As the
stems become long and heavy, they fall out-
wards from the centre, giving the whole plant
a weeping, fern-like appearance. The reddish-
pink, berry-like flowers appear in summer at
the top of long stalks that shoot up from the
centre of the plant. As salad burnet scatters
many seeds which germinate easily, it is advisable to cut the flower heads off as the stalks
begin to lengthen, or it will take over the
garden.

History and mythology

Salad burnet is not well-known today, although it is yet another herb highly regarded
by the ancients. It is thought to have originated in the Mediterranean regions, even
though for a very long time its natural habitat
has been in most of the mountainous areas of
Europe, especially where the conditions are
moist. It was often used as a border plant in
Tudor herb gardens and in knot gardens.

Cultivation

When propagating, sow the seed in spring
(and autumn in temperate climates) where the
plants are to remain. Keep the ground moist
while the seeds are germinating. When seedlings are 8 cm (3 inches) high, thin them out to
30 cm (12 inches) apart. As it is a soft salad herb
and wilts quickly in hot, dry weather, keep the
plants well watered at this time. It has no

particular soil requirements, is very hardy and
will grow strongly all through most winters.

Harvesting and processing

This herb does not dry well for culinary purposes. However, as it is a perennial, fresh
leaves are available throughout the year. If
wishing to dry it for medicinal use, spread leaf
sprays out on a wire rack in a cool, airy place.
When they are brittle and dry, crumble and
store them in airtight containers. For freezing
to go into beverages, pull the small leaves
from the stalks and put them whole into ice
cube trays. Top up with water and freeze.

Various uses

Culinary

Add sprays of salad burnet to a tossed green
salad, or use them as a garnish for sandwiches,
aspics and any dish for a cold buffet. Whole
sprays may also be added to punches, wine
cups, and fruit drinks. When the small leaves
are pulled from the stalks and left whole, they

Salad burnet is a hardy plant and will grow in almost any kind of soil. The fern-like foliage looks most effective if planted as a border.

The leaves of salad burnet have a fresh, cucumber flavour which enhances salads and makes an ideal garnish for sandwiches and buffet dishes.

make an excellent filling for sandwiches, with the addition of a little cream cheese. Or the chopped leaves can be mixed into cream cheese or as a dip.

Medicinal

The Greeks steeped salad burnet leaves in wine cups and other beverages, for like borage, it was said to drive away melancholy. Culpeper endorses this by advising that two or three stalks in a cup of claret will "quicken the spirits" and "refresh and clear the heart". It was also recommended for wounds and was used both inwardly and outwardly. Any part of the herb was considered beneficial for this, the juice, or an infusion, or the powdered root and leaves. Taken as a tea or cordial it is said to promote perspiration and to help cure rheumatism.

Cosmetic

An infusion of salad burnet, cooled and applied to the face regularly, will help clear the skin. A bunch of cucumber-fragrant salad burnet tied in cheesecloth or muslin and put into a hot bath is refreshing and invigorating.

Companion planting

Salad burnet is very nutritious to cattle and sheep and was once grown extensively for this purpose. It has been noted that salad burnet is of particular use to sheep when it is closely cropped, and will give them green feed during the winter when other crops are scarce. In the garden, it mingles especially well with thyme and mint, one early writer pointing out that if these three fragrant herbs are planted together in "alleys", they "perfume the air most delightfully, being trodden on and crushed".

SAVORY

Savory, Winter: *(Satureia montana)*
  Labiatae. Perennial.
Savory, Summer: *(S. hortensis)*
  Labiatae. Annual.
Propagation: *Winter Savory, cuttings, seed. Spring (again in Autumn in temperate climates).*
  Summer Savory, seed. Spring.
Position: *sunny.*
Soil: *light, well drained.*
Height:
  Winter Savory 30 cm (12 inches).
  Summer Savory 60 cm (2 feet).
Part used: *leaves.*

(Left) Winter savory
(Right) Summer savory

Description

Of these two varieties, winter savory is more popular with home gardeners because it is a perennial. The bush is compact with a rather stiff appearance, making it ideal for low hedges to surround small, formal herb beds. The tiny, lipped, white flowers bloom in late summer and autumn. The glossy, green leaves are thin and narrow, and are approximately 12 mm (½ inch) long. The leaves of summer savory are longer and softer and are a bronze-green colour, while the pale pink flowers bloom at the same time as winter savory. The growth habits of the two types are different. Summer savory has slender, erect stems which snap easily and the flavour is stronger than winter savory, which makes it more satisfactory for drying. Most commercial growers prefer it for this reason, and also because the seed can be scattered over large areas with good results in germination. There is a lesser known form of winter savory, *S. repandens*, a decorative prostrate variety whose leaves are smaller and lusher and the white flowers more thickly clustered than those of upright winter savory. However, because of its matted, close form, it is difficult to gather the leaves for culinary use. It spreads in dense, cushiony mounds, making it a desirable plant for filling pockets in rustic paved paths and terraces and in dry stone walls. It is also suitable for planting in hanging baskets, as the low, horizontal habit of the tiny branches will fall over the rim and hang down.

History and mythology

The savories are native to the Mediterranean countries and their history goes back to the remotest times. They were introduced to Britain by the Romans, and later they were among the first herbs taken to the New World by the Pilgrim Fathers. Their botanical name of *satureia* is linked with the satyrs of mythology. Virgil wrote in ancient times that it was amongst the most fragrant of herbs and recommended that it should be grown near bee-hives. Savory vinegar (the leaves steeped in vinegar for some weeks to flavour it) was popular with the Romans. Shakespeare mentions savory several times in his plays:
  "Here's flowers for you;
  Hot lavender, mints, savory, marjoram."
  The Winter's Tale.
Winter savory, when kept neatly clipped, looks attractive as a low hedge to outline knot gardens and was a favourite plant in Tudor days for this purpose.

Cultivation

To propagate winter savory, seed may be sown in spring (and again in autumn in temperate climates) in a prepared seed box, the seedlings to be planted out in a sunny, well drained position when big enough to handle. Another method is to take small tip cuttings of new growth in late spring when the leaves have hardened, then put them in a pot of wet sand until root systems have formed. When setting out in the garden, allow 30 cm (12 inches) between plants. If growing savory as a hedge, put the plants closer together, say about 20 cm (8 inches) apart.

Summer savory is propagated by scattering the seed over finely dug soil where the plants are to remain. Successive sowings may be started in spring and carried on into mid-summer, each crop being harvested just as the flowers begin to appear. When a few centimetres high, prick out the seedlings to approximately 15 cm (6 inches) between plants.

Harvesting and processing

Both savories can be dried with good results by hanging them in bunches in an airy place just before flowering. When leaves are crisp-dry, they are easily separated from the stalks by running the thumb and forefinger up and down the stems. Stored in airtight containers, the flavour will remain strong for a long time. For freezing winter savory, wait for the new soft growth in spring and summer. Summer savory, with its soft foliage, may be frozen at any time. Strip the leaves from their stalks, then chop them finely, mix with a little water and put them into ice cube trays in the freezer. Sprays of fresh winter or summer savory may be wrapped in foil and frozen. It will keep like this for some weeks. Savory butter freezes well, too.

Various uses

Culinary

Both winter and summer savory are used in the same way in food. The finely chopped or dried leaves go with all kinds of cooked beans, either with a little melted butter or in a cream or white sauce. Mix the fresh or dried herb with breadcrumbs for coating fish, pork and veal fillets before frying. It flavours seafood sauces and cocktails and lentil, pea and bean soups. Use savory instead of pepper whenever a pepper flavour is needed.

Medicinal

Winter and summer savory both have strong beneficial properties, and they were once used medicinally for treating colic, flatulence, giddiness and respiratory troubles. Summer

Because of its compact, stiff growth, winter savory makes an excellent low hedge around a formal herb bed. The herb flowers in late summer and autumn.

savory tea is recommended as one of the herbs to help purify the system. In cooking, both savories help digest many foods, especially leguminous vegetables, in particular all varieties of the bean family. Hence its popular German name of *bohnen-kraut*, meaning "bean herb". The sharp, hot flavour of the leaves has also earned it the name of "pepper herb", and it is worthwhile noting that it may be used instead of pepper in the diet where this is desirable.

Cosmetic

Either savory has a tonic and stimulating effect on the skin and may be infused in a muslin or cheesecloth bag in a hot bath for this purpose. An infusion of summer or winter savory freshens the mouth and sweetens the breath. As summer savory tea helps cleanse the system, it has been recorded that it also improves the complexion, making it clear and fresh.

Companion planting

It has been noted that savory seeds inhibit the germination of other seeds when planted nearby. Summer savory is helpful to onions when grown in a border around them. Both summer and winter savories help beans to grow better in the vegetable garden, (as well as being the traditional herb to eat with them). If you are stung by a bee while working in the garden, an old cure is to rub the spot with fresh savory leaves after removing the sting. Honey bees are attracted in swarms to savory when it is in bloom.

SORREL, FRENCH

(Rumex scutatus) Polygonaceae.
  Perennial.

Propagation: *seed, root division.*
  Spring (again in Autumn in mild
  climates).
Position: *sun, or semi-shade.*
Soil: *average, light.*
Height: *45 cm (1½ feet).*
Part used: *leaves.*

Description

There are several species of sorrel, most of
which are found growing wild. These kinds
are very sour and acid-tasting. The variety
known as French sorrel is milder in flavour
and is the type cultivated for culinary use.
French sorrel grows in thick clumps like
spinach. The broad, oval leaves are approximately 15 cm (6 inches) long and 8 cm (3 inches)
wide, and are joined to reddish stems,
resembling a thin rhubarb. The small, greenish flowers appear in summer, near the top,
and on either side, of long, scarlet-streaked
stalks.

History and mythology

French sorrel is native to the South of France,
Switzerland, Italy and Germany, and is closely
related to mountain sorrel, sheep's sorrel,
English or garden sorrel and to the dock
family. Long ago, all these plants were valued
salad and pot-herbs, and were once gathered
wherever they were found growing wild, to
be taken home and put into bubbling stew-
pots, or mixed with other green leaves, for
salads. Sorrel has a reputation for sharpening
the appetite and was highly regarded in the
time of Henry VIII. John Evelyn thought
much of its addition to salads, saying that it:
" . . .imparts a grateful quickness to the rest as
supplying the want of oranges and lemons . . ."

Cultivation

Plants can be cultivated by sowing seed in a
prepared box in spring (and in autumn in mild

climates). When seedlings are big enough to
handle, they should be planted out, leaving
15 cm (6 inches) between each one. Alternatively, seed can be sown directly into the
ground where the plants are to grow, then
thinned out later to 15 cm (6 inches) apart.
Root division of the clumps in the autumn is
also a satisfactory method of increasing French
sorrel. In summer, as soon as the flower-stalks
begin to rise, they should be cut off at the base
to prevent the plant from going to seed. If this
is done, sorrel will continue to flourish for
many years. A small application of manure is
beneficial occasionally and keeping the plants
watered in dry weather is a necessity. Watch
for snails before they eat away the young,
succulent leaves. Caterpillars too, are fond of
this plant.

Harvesting and processing

The fresh leaves are available throughout the
year in moderate climates, so drying should
not be necessary. However, if wishing to dry
them, place freshly picked, unblemished
leaves flat on a wire rack in a cool, dark place

French sorrel has small, greenish flowers which grow on long stalks. These stalks should be removed as soon as they appear to stop the herb from going to seed.

In moderate climates the broad, oval leaves of French sorrel are available throughout the year.

where the air can circulate around them. Store in airtight containers. Whole, washed young sorrel leaves may be carefully wrapped in foil, sealed down with the fingers at the edges and deep frozen for some weeks. Sorrel sauce may also go into the deep freeze packed in sealed containers, then thawed before using. Another method, which was published in an old French cookery book of 1796 (and which I have not tested myself, but considered a good idea), was to preserve the leaves by cooking them over a slow fire with salt and butter until all moisture had evaporated. When half cold, the sorrel was pressed into pots. When quite cold, tepid melted butter was poured over the top and the pots were sealed down and kept in a dry place. Once opened, the contents would not keep for more than three weeks.

Various uses

Culinary

Formerly, one of the favourite culinary uses for sorrel was to cook and eat it like spinach, with the addition of well-beaten eggs and butter, or cream, to mellow the sharp flavour. Another well-known use for French sorrel, still popular today, is in soup. Sorrel sauce is a delicious accompaniment for cold poultry, fish gelatine moulds, hot boiled potatoes and as a filling for omelettes. Tender shortloin lamb chops, or lamb cutlets, bathed in a thin sorrel sauce are delicious. The young leaves torn into a tossed green salad give a pleasant, appetizing bite.

N.B. Sorrel, like spinach, should not be cooked in aluminium.

Medicinal

Sorrel leaves were eaten to assist the kidneys and digestion. They were made into a spring tonic for the blood and a cooling drink for fevers. As there is some oxalic acid present in the plant, the leaves should not be eaten too frequently. Culpeper writes: "...it is useful to cool inflammation and heat of the blood in agues, pestilential or choleric, or sickness and fainting, arising from the heart; to quench thirst and procure an appetite in fainting or decaying stomachs..." Indeed, sorrel leaves were often eaten by country folk to allay thirst, although it would have been one of the various wild sorrels and not the cultivated French sorrel.

Cosmetic

Sorrel contains calcium and because of this is listed as one of the herbs which retard the signs of old age, helping to keep the skin firm and wrinkle-free. Many herbs are recommended for use in a facial steam, different herbs being suited to various skin types. Sorrel is suggested for dry, sensitive skins. Sorrel is also one of the herbs used in herbal cosmetics for healing acne. I have used an astringent cream based on sorrel. It is also recommended to be taken as a tea to help clear the skin.

Companion planting

We have found in our own herb garden, that French sorrel has been growing happily in three large clumps for twenty years next to oregano; the oregano almost engulfing the sorrel. Neither herb has had any disease and they are exceptionally healthy plants. Snails and caterpillars are the worst enemies of sorrel.

TARRAGON, FRENCH

(Artemisia dracunculus) Compositeae.
  Perennial.
Propagation: *cuttings, root division.*
  Late Spring cuttings, early Spring
  division.
Position: *sunny*
Soil: *light, well drained.*
Height: *90 cm (3 feet)*
Part used: *leaves*

Description

French tarragon, with its unique, tart flavour and spicy aroma, is one of the most sought after culinary herbs. The leaves are long and narrow and grow on either side of thin, wiry stalks which, together with the main stems, twist and fall in a tangled way, forming a thick, bushy plant 90 cm (3 feet) high. Small, tight, yellowish buds appear in late summer, which rarely open into full bloom, therefore they do not set seed. There is another variety which is grown from seed called Russian tarragon, a native of Siberia. At first glance it resembles French tarragon, but on closer inspection you can see that the foliage is bigger, with pronounced indentations here and there on the leaves. This species has very little flavour, although when French tarragon is hard to find, Russian tarragon in greater quantities, can be used as a substitute in a recipe. Recently, we have come across another form of tarragon, which our relatives and friends in England insist on calling French tarragon. It is also known as "winter tarragon" and it has been given the botanical name of *Tagetes Lucida.* It is a sturdier, neater looking plant than French tarragon, with firm, dark green leaves, and best of all, a strong, spicy aroma and flavour which is typical of true French tarragon. It has bright yellow flowers which set seed. If you cannot find French tarragon, winter tarragon is a substitute worth growing.

History and mythology

French tarragon is native to the Mediterranean countries, and has long been popular in Conti-

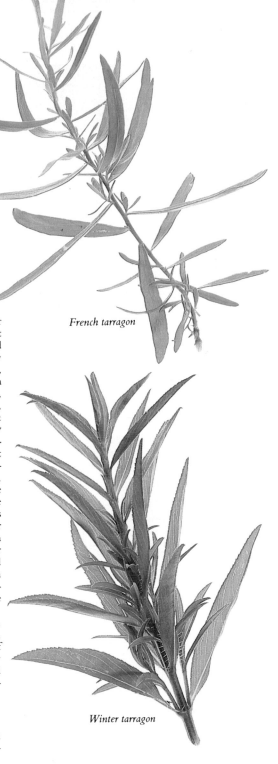

French tarragon

Winter tarragon

French tarragon grows into a thick, bushy plant.

Winter tarragon has yellow flowers which set seed.

nental cookery. The name tarragon is adapted from the French word *estragon*, meaning "little dragon" There is a strange old legend about the origin of tarragon (unsubstantiated but quaint) that says the seed of flax put into a radish root, or a sea onion, and set in the ground, brought forth this herb! It was also recorded that it cured the bites and stings of reptiles, venomous insects and mad dogs.

Cultivation

To obtain a large quantity of new French tarragon plants, propagating by cuttings is advised. Take 15 cm (6 inch) tip cuttings in late spring when the new, soft leaves have become fairly firm. Insert the cuttings, which have had the lower leaves carefully removed, in a pot of coarse river sand, leaving approximately 5 cm (2 inches) of the cuttings above the sand. By mid-summer the roots should have become established enough for planting out. Allow 30 cm (12 inches) between plants. Propagating from root division will not yield as many plants, but is satisfactory for a limited number. The plant dies away to ground level in winter, (except in very warm climates), new shoots appearing early in the spring from a creeping root system. At this time, sever pieces of the main root 5 cm (2 inches) long, together with a new shoot, and plant 30 cm (12 inches) apart. Within about two months these root cuttings are roughly 45 cm (1½ feet)

high. Although this herb needs well drained soil and a sunny position, it also needs to be kept watered, especially in dry weather. In severely cold climates, keep the roots covered in winter with grass clippings or straw.

Harvesting and processing

As tarragon withers away in winter and there are no fresh leaves to pick then, it is important to preserve them when they are in abundance. For drying, harvesting may be started in summer just as the flower buds appear, and continued from time to time until late autumn before the leaves begin to turn yellow. Hang the leafy stalks in bunches, or spread them out on wire racks for quicker drying, in a cool, airy place. When dry, strip the leaves from the stalks and store them in airtight containers away from the light. For freezing, strip the fresh leaves from their stalks, chop finely, mix with a little water and put them into ice cube trays in the freezer. Sprays of tarragon may be wrapped in foil and frozen for some weeks. Finely chopped tarragon blended into softened butter, allowed to harden, then cut into squares and sealed in polythene bags or foil may be frozen too.

Various uses

Culinary

French tarragon is one of the four essential

As French tarragon leaves are not available in the winter months, it is important that they are gathered and preserved while they are in abundance.

ingredients in the "fines herbes" mixture, (the others being chives, chervil and parsley; each of these herbs having their own delicate and individual flavour and texture, which when put together in equal quantities make a delicious and subtle combination). It is interesting to note that of all the *artemisia* group, tarragon is the only one which has culinary uses. The others, such as wormwood and southernwood, are much too bitter to eat, although they have their place among the medicinal herbs. The warming, aromatic fragrance of tarragon complements fish and shellfish, the fresh leaves being especially useful for decorating and flavouring fish moulds. It is an excellent herb to use with chicken, turkey, game, veal, liver, kidneys, egg dishes and in chicken or fish soups. Tarragon can be added to a sour cream dressing, mayonnaise, a melted butter sauce, French dressing, tartare sauce, Béarnaise sauce and to a green salad. Tarragon steeped in white vinegar gives it a particularly savoury flavour.

Medicinal

This herb has long been respected as a source of "warmth forces". Culpeper says the leaves are "heating and drying" and John Evelyn says that it is "highly cordial and friend of the head, heart and liver". The leaves contain an exceptionally high quantity of warm, volatile oils, which is why it was advised to mix them with other herbs and with lettuce, that they may "temper the coldness" of a salad.

Cosmetic

Tarragon is one of the few herbs that appear to have no contribution to make in the cosmetic field, although many herbal soaps today contain extracts and oils from nearly all the herbs, both culinary and scented. Oil of tarragon would be a fragrant addition to a beauty soap.

Companion planting

Tarragon is one of the aromatic herbs that are generally helpful to the other plants in the garden, and does not appear to hinder the formation of seed, or the growth, of any herbs or vegetables.

THYME

Thyme, Garden: *(Thymus vulgaris)*
    Labiatae. Perennial.
Thyme, Lemon: *(T. citriodorus)*
    Labiatae. Perennial.
Propagation: *seed, cuttings, root*
    division. Spring.
Position: *open, sunny*
Soil: *light, sandy.*
Height: *23 cm (9 inches)-30 cm*
    (12 inches).
Part used: *leaves.*

Description

Of all the numerous varieties of thyme,
garden and lemon thyme are the two kinds
which have the most value in cooking. Certain
ornamental varieties, like Westmoreland
thyme, golden, variegated lemon thyme, and
pretty, grey Silver Posie may be used in emer-
gencies, but their flavour is not as pungent nor
as true. There are also a number of creeping,
mat-like species, but they have such inter-
woven, tiny branches, that the tedious job of
trying to disentangle a sufficient quantity for
cooking is simply not worthwhile. Garden
thyme has very small greyish-green leaves
which are joined to thin stalks projecting in an
angular fashion from hard, woody stems that
form an erect, bushy plant 30 cm (12 inches)
high. The flowers are pinkish-white and appear
in spring in whorls at the tips of the branches.
Lemon thyme has slightly larger and greener
leaves than garden thyme and the spring-
blooming flowers are deep pink. It has a
spreading type of habit and only grows to
about 15 cm (6 inches) high. When the foliage
is crushed, an unmistakable lemony fragrance
overlaying the typical thyme scent is released.
This makes it valuable for giving a more subtle
flavour to food where required.

History and mythology

The *thymus* family is indigenous to the
Mediterranean lands, and people declare that it
grows with more flavour in its native soil than
anywhere else. The tiny, pungent leaves have
a primitive form, their outward simplicity
belying the great beneficial forces within.
Thyme has antiseptic qualities, the name in its
Greek form was a derivative of a word mean-

(Left) Garden thyme
(Right) Lemon thyme

*Variegated lemon
thyme*

Lemon thyme

Westmoreland thyme is grown as a decorative garden herb rather than for use in the kitchen.

Grey woolly thyme is another variety which is not used in cooking but makes a very attractive border.

Silver posie thyme is as pretty as its name and again this is not a herb which is grown for eating.

Cat thyme has a creeping, mat-like growth habit and makes an excellent ornamental groundcover.

ing "to fumigate". Others say the name comes from the Greek word *thumus*, signifying courage. The ancient Romans liked the aromatic flavour thyme gave to cheese and to the various alcoholic beverages they made. It was a loved plant in Elizabethan times and was used extensively in garden borders. Shakespeare wrote of herbs many times and obviously appreciated their qualities: "I know a bank whereon the wild thyme blows" is a favourite line from *A Midsummer Night's Dream*. Herb writers of old have told us that "Wild thyme has always been a favourite with fairies".

Cultivation

For garden thyme, the seeds, which are extremely small, can be sown in spring into a prepared seed box, or they can be scattered straight into finely dug soil, kept moist, and thinned out later to about 15 cm (6 inches)

between plants. Propagating by root division is another satisfactory procedure and should also be done in spring. Divide the bush into as many pieces as required, making sure each piece has some good rootlets attached, and firm them into the ground. Alternatively, garden thyme can be propagated by taking tip cuttings approximately 10 cm (4 inches) long in late spring, inserting them into a pot of sand and keeping them watered. This last method ensures good root systems very quickly. Garden thyme, except when young, does not require much watering and no fertilizing at all. Where soil is too poor for cereal crops, garden thyme will grow well and have more flavour

Lemon thyme has a spreading habit and is used in the kitchen.

than pampered, manured plants which may look healthy and lush, but will lack pungency. Cut the bushes back hard at the end of flowering and renew them every two years or so. Propagating lemon thyme from seed is not recommended, as the seedlings cannot be guaranteed to be as strongly fragrant as the parent plant. For this reason, the seed is not readily available in commercial quantities. Propagation is either by tip cuttings or root division, using the same methods as for garden thyme. For healthy plants, cut them back after flowering has finished and start again with fresh plants every two or three years.

Harvesting and processing

For drying both garden and lemon thyme, harvest the leafy branches just before they start to flower for fullest flavour, and gather them on a dry day before midday. Hang them in bunches in a shady, airy place, and when crisp-dry, strip off the leaves and seal in airtight containers. The taste and aroma of both these thymes are much more penetrating when dried. As the foliage of thyme is so tiny, we think it a laborious job to strip the stalks for freezing a few leaves in ice cube trays, when this herb dries so well. Washed and dried sprays of thyme can be sealed in foil and frozen whole for several weeks.

The leaves of lemon thyme are larger than garden thyme and this variety has a deep pink flower.

Various uses

Culinary

The special fragrance of garden thyme enhances many dishes and is also a necessary ingredient in many herb blends, such as mixed herbs (the others being sage and marjoram) and in a bouquet garni, with parsley, marjoram and a bay leaf. The savoury, pungent flavour of garden thyme is indispensable for using in soups, stews, casseroles, meat loaf,

Garden thyme, the only other thyme with culinary uses, has a very small, greyish-green leaf.

rissoles, with all kinds of meat, in stuffings, tasty sauces, marinades, and pâté. It gives savour to herb bread and to many vegetables, such as eggplant, zucchini, marrow, tomatoes, haricot and lima beans, onions and beetroot. Lemon thyme, with its milder flavour, is excellent with fish, chicken or turkey momays, steamed carrots, omelettes and in all kinds of food with a delicate or bland flavour. It is sometimes used as an extra ingredient in a "fines herbes" blend, with chervil, chives, parsley and tarragon.

Medicinal

Thyme is a plant which absorbs sunlight and converts it into potent volatile oils containing substances that have made this herb a valuable medicine for treating coughs, colds, cramps, colic, poor digestion and loss of appetite. As mentioned earlier, the plant also has antiseptic qualities. Herbalists also recommend thyme tea for relieving headaches, bowel and bladder disorders, as a nerve tonic and for toning up the reproductive system. As with sage, it is said to improve the eyesight and clear the brain. Because of its powerful antiseptic qualities, herbalists sometimes recommend thyme to be used with sage (good for afflictions of the mouth and throat) as a gargle for sore throats.

Cosmetic

Thyme is used today in herbal toothpastes, mouth washes and natural deodorants. It is also used in soaps and herbal bath salts and in facial tonics as it tones up the skin. Thyme may also be used in a facial steam for normal skin.

Companion planting

Thyme, as one of the most aromatic of all herbs, has a beneficial effect in the garden and associates well with lavender. It helps repel cabbage root fly, and when dried, acts as a moth repellent in cupboards and drawers. Bees have always loved this herb when in flower, and honey made from it is the most delicious and fragrant of all. Thyme was always planted near the bee-hives and the hives were also rubbed with it.

SOMETHING OLD, SOMETHING NEW

The cultivation of herbs is one of
the most pleasurable and
rewarding types of gardening.
In addition to enhancing your
home and garden with their
beauty and fragrance, fresh herbs
have many practical uses.
The following are some of our
favourite recipes.

THE RECIPES

Woodcut from title page of 'Grete Herball' (1526).

Sorrel soup

Serves: 4
Cooking time: 1¼–1½ hours (approx.)

125 g (4 oz) butter or vegetable margarine
1 small bunch, 125 g (4 oz) sorrel leaves, shredded
8 cups water
500 g (1 lb) potatoes, washed, peeled and diced
1–2 teaspoons salt
pepper to taste
2 egg yolks

Melt the butter in a saucepan, stir in the shredded sorrel and simmer until softened. Add water, potatoes, salt and pepper. Bring to the boil, then simmer with the lid on for 1 hour. Press the soup through a sieve, or purée in a blender. Reheat in the saucepan. Blend a little of the hot liquid into the beaten egg yolks, pour into the saucepan of soup and stir well without boiling. Chill. Serve with a spoonful of cream in each bowl and a little chopped parsley. Serve hot in winter.

Note: Recipe was previously published in Rosemary Hemphill's *Herbs For All Seasons*

Green cress soup

Serves: 4
Cooking time: 1½ hours (approx.)

500 g (1 lb) potatoes, peeled and diced
2 green outside lettuce leaves, chopped
1 onion, peeled and chopped
2½ cups water
2 cups milk
1 cup firmly packed cress leaves, any variety, chopped finely
2 teaspoons salt

Simmer potatoes, lettuce and onion with water in a covered saucepan for 1 hour. Purée soup in a blender or press through a sieve, return to saucepan on a low heat. In a separate pot, heat milk, then stir into purée until thoroughly blended. Add cress and salt, remove from stove and serve. For cold cress soup, chill in refrigerator, pour into cold glasses or bowls, top with a spoonful of sour cream and a cress leaf.

Beetroot in caraway port jelly

Serves: 8-10

1 bunch beetroot
2 teaspoons salt
½ cup sweet port wine
3 tablespoons lemon juice
2 teaspoons honey

1 teaspoon caraway seed
3 rounded teaspoons gelatine

Cut the tops off the beetroot, putting any unblemished leaves aside to use later in salads or in soups. Wash the beets well and place in a saucepan with salt and enough water to cover. Simmer until tender. Peel beets, cut them into dice, circles or quarters and arrange in a dish. Measure 1½ cups of the liquid and return to the saucepan on a low heat with the port, lemon juice, honey and caraway seed, adding more salt if necessary. Pour some of the hot liquid onto the gelatine, stir until clear, pour back into the saucepan and stir again, then cover the cut up beets with the tasty, crimson broth. Cool, then chill in refrigerator until set.

Horseradish sauce

1 cup white sauce
pinch mustard powder
pinch salt
pinch sugar
2 teaspoons lemon juice
1 tablespoon cream
2 tablespoons freshly grated horseradish, or 1 tablespoon
dried horseradish grains

White sauce:
3 tablespoons butter
3 tablespoons plain flour
3 cups milk
salt and freshly ground pepper

Make sauce by melting butter in a saucepan, blending in plain flour, adding milk and salt and pepper to taste. Stir until thickened. Add remaining ingredients to sauce and mix thoroughly. If using dried horseradish, leave sauce for 1 hour before serving.

Pawpaw seed dressing with parsley

Here is an adaptation from Hawaii of an unusual and healthy salad dressing featuring pawpaw seeds. These peppery seeds have a traditional reputation for assisting the digestion. An added advantage is knowing that you are going to use most of those glistening black seeds when cutting open a pawpaw, instead of scooping them out and throwing them away. Vitamin-rich parsley and tasty spices go towards making this dressing a delectable flavour treat.

2 teaspoons sugar
½ teaspoon salt
3–4 tablespoons lemon juice (according to taste)
1 tablespoon onion, chopped
½ teaspoon crushed garlic

1 tablespoon freshly chopped parsley, chervil or dill leaves
1 cup any cold pressed salad oil (walnut oil makes an interesting change)
2 tablespoons fresh pawpaw seeds

Place all dry ingredients and lemon juice in blender. Gradually add salad oil while blending. When thoroughly blended add pawpaw seeds. Blend again until seeds are the size of coarse ground pepper. Store dressing in sealed container in the refrigerator.

Pestou

This delectable recipe for pestou (or pesto) was given to us by Mrs Clare Wilmot of the Triad Health Clinic, who has presented us with a jar many times from her freezer. We have eaten it with relish as a spread, and it has various other uses as well, including folding it through cooked, drained hot spaghetti.

1 large bunch sweet basil
125 g (4 oz) Parmesan cheese
125 g (4 oz) pine kernels
4 cloves garlic, peeled
a little sea salt
oil

Place all ingredients in a blender with sufficient oil to give the mixture the consistency of thick, running cream. Blend thoroughly. Use immediately or store in a suitable container in the refrigerator.

Baked broccoli with dill seed and sour cream

Serves:4
Cooking time: 20-30 minutes
Oven temperature: 180°C (350°F)

500 g (1 lb) broccoli, cooked or 1 small cauliflower, cooked
2 teaspoons dill seed
salt and pepper
1 cup sour cream
1 cup breadcrumbs
green dill for garnish

Place cooked broccoli (or cooked cauliflower) in an ovenproof dish. Sprinkle with dill seed, dust with salt and pepper, cover with sour cream, and top with breadcrumbs. Bake in a moderate oven 180°C (350°F) until crumbs are brown. Garnish with a few sprays of green dill if available.

Rosemary zucchini

Serves: 4
Cooking time: 10 minutes (approx.)

500 g (1 lb) zucchini
1 tomato, peeled and chopped
1 tablespoon finely chopped onion
2 teaspoons finely chopped rosemary
salt and pepper
2 tablespoons vegetable oil

Thinly slice the zucchini and place in a saucepan with tomato, onion, rosemary, salt, pepper and vegetable oil. Cover and simmer gently until soft, stirring frequently in the beginning to prevent the vegetables from sticking.

Healthy brown rice and mint salad

Serves: 6

2 cups brown rice, cooked
1 cup raw slivered almonds, browned in oven
2 medium-size ripe tomatoes, peeled and chopped
½ teaspoon salt
1 tablespoon finely chopped onion or shallots
2 tablespoons finely chopped mint
4 tablespoons finely chopped parsley
4 tablespoons lemon juice
4 tablespoons vegetable oil

Mix all the ingredients together in the order given. Serve.

French beans and savory

Serves:4

500 g (1 lb) French beans
½ teaspoon salt
2 teaspoons finely chopped savory
2 teaspoons finely chopped shallots or onion
4 tablespoons sour cream

Cook prepared French beans in water until tender. Drain. To the beans in the saucepan add salt, savory, shallots or onion, and sour cream. Steam gently with the lid on until heated through. Serve hot.

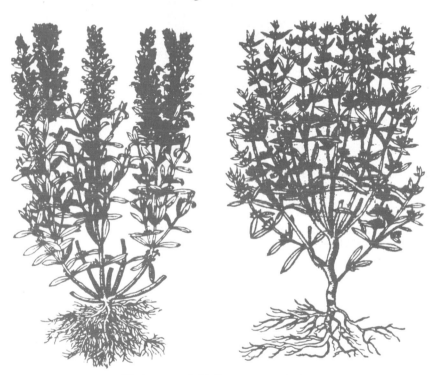

Winter savory (left) Summer savory (right)
from 'The Herball' (1597)

Comfrey fritters

comfrey leaves
batter

Strip the comfrey leaves from the plant. Dip them in cold water, then into batter. Fry in sizzling fat to make unusual, but delicous fritters.

Chicken salad

Serves: 2

½ cup natural yoghurt
¼ teaspoon dry mustard
1 teaspoon lemon juice
½ teaspoon garlic salt
dash of pepper
1 tablespoon chopped chives
2 teaspoons chopped sage
1 cup diced cooked chicken

½ green cucumber, peeled and diced
lettuce leaves

In a bowl stir together yoghurt, mustard, lemon juice, garlic, salt, pepper, chives and sage. Fold into this mixture cold diced chicken and cucumber Serve the salad in crisp, curved lettuce leaves.

Sage welsh rarebit

Serves: 2
Cooking time: 20 minutes (approx.)

1 tablespoon cornflour
½ cup beer
1 cup grated cheddar cheese
hot buttered toast
1 tablespoon butter
2 teaspoons finely chopped sage
salt and pepper

Blend the cornflour and beer together until smooth, put into a saucepan together with the cheese, butter, sage, salt and pepper. Stir continually over a gentle heat until melted and thickened. Do not overcook. Pour immediately over toast.

Brown bread herb sandwiches

Fresh, green, finely chopped herbs make delicous and nourishing fillings for sandwiches. Brown, wholemeal or any other health bread is recommended. To help bring out the flavour of the herbs, first spread a thin film of vegemite or cream cheese onto the buttered bread. Pick the herbs, wash them and strip the leaves from the stalks (except for those with soft stems like salad burnet) and chop very finely. Always fill the sandwiches generously with the herbs, slice crusts off the bread, and cut into triangles or squares. These sandwiches can be made in advance, wrapped in plastic or foil, and refrigerated. Serve for morning or afternoon tea, or as accompaniment to soups, entrées, or luncheon and supper dishes. There are no rules about which herbs to use either singly or mixed, it is a matter of individual taste, although it is best not to have too many strong flavours together. Mild, fragrant herbs make a background for a dominant herb.

Sandwich filling:
Pick several sprays each of parsley, chives, marjoram, salad burnet and tarragon, two leaves of eau–de–Cologne mint and one sage leaf. Chop them all together. The dominant herb is tarragon.

Curried egg mousse

Serves: 6 for lunch
10 for entrée

1 x 430 g (15 oz) can chilled evaporated milk
1 x 430 g (15 oz) can cream-type soup (e.g. celery, asparagus,
vichysoisse, watercress)
1 tablespoon curry powder
2 teaspoons onion powder
1 tablespoon lemon or lime juice
1 tablespoon gelatine melted in a little hot water
8 hard-boiled eggs, chopped
salt to taste
1 tablespoon chopped parsley or chives
2 tarragon or dill leaves
Garnish: 1 small jar caviare or lump-fish roe and 1 lime or lemon

Whip ½ can evaporated milk until thick. Put remainder of milk into blender together with soup, curry powder, onion powder, lime or lemon juice, melted gelatine and roughly chopped eggs. Blend until smooth. Fold this mixture, with parsley, into whipped milk. Add salt to taste. Pour into wetted mould and set in refrigerator. When set, unmould and spread caviare on top. Surround mousse with thinly sliced lime or lemon and sprigs of fresh herbs. Serve with a tossed salad (and cold meat if you wish). This dish can be accompanied by a bowl of chutney.

Fennel bulbs with cheese sauce

Serves: 4
For a light lunch.

Trim and wash 2 fennel bulbs, cut in halves and simmer in boiling water for 20 minutes. Drain well, then lay the bulbs cut side down in an ovenproof dish and pour 1 cup of white sauce over them. (Some finely chopped fennel leaves stirred into the sauce first is an excellent addition.) Sprinkle 2 tablespoons of grated tasty cheese over the top and place under the griller until the cheese has melted. Serve hot.

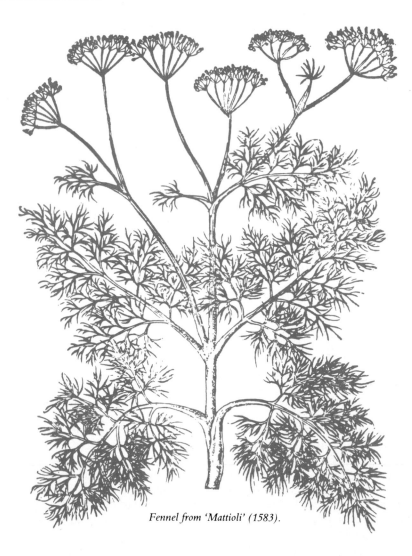

Fennel from 'Mattioli' (1583).

Chicory casserole

Serves: 4
Cooking time: 1½ hours
Oven temperature: 150°C (300°F)

4 chicory heads
butter or vegetable margarine
2 teaspoons dried thyme
salt and pepper

Wash and trim the chicory. Cut it into circles and pack into a buttered casserole dish with the thyme, salt, pepper and pieces of butter between the layers. Put the lid on and bake in a moderate oven, 150°C (300°F) for about 1½ hours.

Tomato and bergamot loaf

Serves: 4
Cooking time: 20 minutes
Oven temperature: 180°C (350°F)

1½ cups canned tomatoes with juice
2 tablespoons water
2 tablespoons chopped bergamot leaves
1 cup celery, chopped
1½ cups package breadcrumbs
1 cup grated tasty cheese
2 tablespoons vegetable oil
2 tablespoons onion, grated
½ teaspoon salt
2 eggs, beaten

Break up tomatoes and mix together with all the ingredients in the order given, spoon into an oiled ovenproof dish and bake in a moderate oven 180°C (350°F) for 20 minutes. Serve hot.

Garlic bread

You will probably have to cut the loaf in half as there are not many ovens long enough to hold an unbroken French loaf. With a sharp knife, cut the bread in slices almost to the bottom, being careful not to sever the slices. Peel and crush garlic, mash thoroughly into the butter. Spread garlic butter generously on both sides of bread slices. Wrap loosely in aluminium foil, place in a hot oven for 10–15 minutes, until bread is crisp and golden. Serve hot, each person tearing off their own slices.
Note: Parsley and other herbs can be added to the basic garlic butter.

Thick oxtail and lentil stew

Serves: 6
This is a tasty and nourishing cold weather dish.
Cooking time: 3 hours

2 cut oxtails
2 tablespoons flour
2 tablespoons vegetable oil
6 cups water
½ teaspoon each peppercorns and juniper berries
2 bay leaves
a branch of garden thyme
2 cloves of garlic, chopped
½ cup green lentils
3 teaspoons salt
1 large carrot, chopped
1 small turnip, chopped
2 onions, chopped
2 stalks celery, chopped
parsley for garnish

Roll oxtails in flour, then brown all over in a saucepan in the oil. Add water and bring to the boil with the lid on. Add peppercorns, juniper berries, bay leaves, thyme, garlic, lentils and salt. Lower heat, cover and simmer for 2 hours, skimming off the fat as it rises to the surface. Add all the vegetables and simmer for another hour. Sprinkle chopped parsley over each helping. Serve with steaming–hot boiled potatoes.

Aioli

12 garlic cloves, peeled
salt
3 egg yolks
1¾ cups best olive oil
a few drops lemon juice

Mash the garlic cloves to a cream on a board with a little salt, using a sharp knife, then transfer to a bowl. Stir in the egg yolks with a wooden spoon, and when well blended start beating in the oil drop by drop. As the mixture thickens, and when about half the oil has been used, add the rest of the oil a little more quickly, in a steady stream, still beating. Add the lemon juice last. If the aioli separates — and this applies to any mayonnaise — put a fresh yolk in another bowl and slowly add the curdled sauce to it.

Note: Recipe was previously published in Rosemary Hemphill's *Herbs For All Seasons*.

Chicken and parsley pie

Serves: 6-8

1 × 2 kg (4 lb) chicken
3 teaspoons salt
bouquet garni, fresh, *or* 2 teaspoons prepared dried mixture
3 tablespoons butter or vegetable margarine
4 tablespoons plain flour
4 tablespoons finely chopped parsley
2 tablespoons finely chopped onion
6 hard boiled eggs, sliced
2 cups mashed pototo

Simmer the chicken until tender in enough water to come half-way up the sides of the bird, with salt and bouquet garni. Remove chicken, slice meat away from bones, discard skin. Skim fat off reserved stock, (there should be at least 3 cups of stock; if not, top up with water). Make a sauce with the butter, flour and stock, then stir in onion and 3 tablespoons of parsley. Put a layer of chicken in an ovenproof dish, then half the eggs and half the sauce, repeat with the same ingredients. Mash 1 tablespoon of parsley into the potato and spread over the top. Heat and serve.

Roast tarragon chicken

Serves: 4
Cooking time: 1½ hours
Oven temperature: 190°C (375°F)

1 × 2 kg (4 lb) chicken
salt and pepper
knob butter
bunch tarragon, or 3 teaspoons dried tarragon
4 tablespoons vegetable oil
2 bacon rashers

Wash chicken and shake salt and pepper into the cavity, add a knob of butter and a bunch of tarragon (or 2 teaspoons of dried tarragon). Place the bird in a baking dish, pour vegetable oil over it, sprinkle with salt and pepper, and put a spray of tarragon, or 1 teaspoon dried tarragon, on top. Place greaseproof paper, or a piece of brown paper, over the chicken and put it in a moderately hot oven, 190°C (375°F) for 1½ hours. After 20-30 minutes, take the paper off the bird, baste it with the liquid from the dish, then replace paper. If roasting vegetables, put them into the baking dish now with the chicken. Baste again in another ½ hour. During the last 20 minutes of cooking, remove the paper and cover the breast with bacon rashers. Serve hot with gravy and the roast vegetables.

Salmon and marjoram pie

Serves: 4-6
Cooking time: 35–40 minutes (approx.)
Oven temperature: 180°C (350°F)

4 cups soft breadcrumbs
3 tablespoons butter
3 tablespoons plain flour
3 cups milk
salt and freshly ground pepper
juice of lemon
1 × 440 g (14 oz) can flaked salmon
1 × 440 g (14 oz) asparagus cuts, drained
6 hard boiled eggs, sliced
1 tablespoon finely chopped marjoram
1 tablespoon finely chopped parsley
2 tablespoons cheese, grated

Breadcrumb Case: Toss 3 cups of soft breadcrumbs in melted butter until well coated. Reserve 1 cup for later, and press the rest firmly into the shape of an ovenproof plate. Brown in a moderate oven, 180°C (350°F) for 5-10 minutes.

Filling: Make a white sauce by melting butter in a saucepan, blend in plain flour, add milk, salt and pepper to taste. Stir until thickened. Add the lemon juice, flaked salmon, drained asparagus cuts, eggs, marjoram and parsley. Pour into crumb case, top with the reserved buttered crumbs and 2 tablespoons of grated cheese. Bake in a moderate oven 180°C (350°F) until heated through and cheese is melted.

Sweet marjoram (left) Pot marjoram (right)
from 'The Herball' (1597)

Herbed leg of lamb

Serves: 6
Cooking time: 3½ hours (approx.)
Oven temperature: 160°C (325°F)

This unusual and delicious recipe was given to us by Gretta Anna Teplitzky, a good friend and a gifted cook.

1 × 2 kg (4 lb) leg of lamb
salt and pepper
4 cloves garlic, peeled and cut into slivers
10 sprigs thyme
10 sprigs rosemary
juice of 2 lemons (optional)
1 cup vegetable oil, or good beef fat

Sprinkle salt and pepper all over the lamb. Make small incisions in the meat with a pointed knife, and press the garlic slivers into them. Place 5 sprigs each of thyme and rosemary in the bottom of a roasting pan and lay the leg on the herbs. Place 5 more sprigs each of thyme and rosemary on top of the lamb, and pour over the lemon juice and the oil. Place in a slow oven 160°C (325°F), for about 3½ hours. (The meat should be just pink where it touches the bone.) Remove lamb to a serving platter, decorating it with all the cooked herb sprigs. Pour off the fat from the baking dish, leaving the essence or juice for making gravy in the usual manner. The joint is brought to the table with the herbs on top, but they are pushed to one side when carving, and are not served.

Macaroni with sour cream and oregano

Serves: 4-6
Cooking time: 30 minutes (approx.)
Oven temperature: 180°C (350°F)

250 g (8 oz) elbow macaroni
1 cup dairy sour cream
4 eggs, separated
1 tablespoon finely chopped oregano
salt and pepper
1 tablespoon black olives, pitted and chopped

Cook and drain macaroni. Combine sour cream and lightly beaten yolks, season with salt and pepper, add macaroni, oregano and olives. Whip whites and fold into mixture. Bake in a greased ovenproof dish in a moderate oven, 180°C (350°F) for approximately 30 minutes. The mixture should not be dry, but slightly soft in the centre.

Salmon and basil loaf

Serves: 5-6
Cooking time: 45 minutes
Oven temperature: 180°C (350°F)

2 × 440 g cans red salmon, flaked
1 cup dry breadcrumbs
4 tablespoons tomato paste
1 green pepper, finely chopped
1 onion, finely chopped
½ teaspoon salt
1 tablespoon finely chopped basil
4 eggs, beaten
3 tablespoons vegetable oil

Mash all the ingredients, except the oil, together in a bowl in the order given above. Grease a loaf tin and pack the mixture into it, then refrigerate for a few hours. Loosen the edges with a knife, turn the loaf into a shallow ovenproof dish, and pour the oil over it. Bake in a moderate oven 180°C (350°F) for 45 minutes. Serve hot with the following sauce.

Tomato sauce: Stew 4 medium sized peeled tomatoes in a little butter with salt, pepper and a pinch of sugar and some basil, then thicken with a tablespoon of cornflour smoothed in a little milk. Serve hot in a jug separately.

Sweet basil (left) Bush basil (right)
from 'The Herball' (1597)

Minted honey soufflé

Serves: 4

½ cup clear honey
½ teaspoon ground coriander seed
spray of spearmint (or ¼ teaspoon dried mint)
crystallized mint leaves (page 114)
4 eggs, separated
½ cup milk
4 teaspoons gelatine, dissolved in hot water
½ cup cream, whipped

Place honey and coriander in the top half of a double saucepan over boiling water. Beat yolks and milk together, blend with the honey, using a wooden spoon. Add the sprig of mint, and continue stirring until custard coats the spoon. Remove from heat, add melted gelatine. Cool custard by replacing hot water in the boiler with several changes of cold water, stirring constantly. When cooled, remove mint, and fold in the whipped cream and stiffly beaten egg whites. Turn into a serving bowl and chill in refrigerator. When set, spread whipped cream over the top and decorate with crystallized mint leaves.

Spiced whole grapes

A delicious accompaniment to grills, baked meat, poultry, fish or curry.

1 kg (2 lb) seedless white grapes

500 g (1 lb) raw sugar
142 ml (4 fl oz) cider or white vinegar
2 teaspoons mustard seed
1 teaspoon ground ginger
1 teaspoon ground allspice
2 bay leaves
30 g (1 oz) powdered fruit pectin

Wash grapes and remove stalks. Place sugar and vinegar in a saucepan and add mustard seed, ginger, allspice and bay leaves. Bring to boil, then simmer gently, uncovered, for 15 minutes, stirring at intervals. Remove bay leaves. Add grapes, sprinkle in pectin. Bring to boil again and simmer for further 3 minutes, skimming off any foam and giving the mixture an occasional stir. Remove from heat and allow to stand for 10 minutes, stirring frequently to prevent a film from forming on the top. Spoon into jars and seal. Use within 4 weeks.

Lavender sachets

These can be made in different shapes, from lace-edged hearts to bags tied with ribbon. The sizes vary from tiny sachets for scattering amongst underclothes or sheets, to larger ones with loops to swing from coat-hangers. Imagination will help you decide on the materials to use, whether of traditional sprigged muslin in pastel shades, or prints in modern, vivid colours, or plain organza in 'sweet-pea' hues of mauve, pink, mist-blue or soft magenta. Dried English lavender flowers are used for filling the sachets, or a pot-pourri mixture for 'sweet bags'.

Pot-pourri

4 cups rose petals
2 cups scented geranium leaves
2 cups lavender flowers and leaves
1 cup lemon verbena leaves
2 tablespoons orris root powder
1 teaspoon rose geranium oil
1 teaspoon lavender oil
1 teaspoon ground cloves
1 tablespoon ground cinnamon
several pieces cinnamon bark
12 whole cloves

Follow the directions for drying the flowers and leaves as described in their sections. Take a wide-topped glass jar, or an earthenware crock (do not use a plastic or aluminium container) and put all the flowers and leaves into it, mingling them together. Put the orris powder, ground cloves and cinnamon into a small bowl and blend, then add the essential oils, combining them into the powder. Add the mixed powder to the dried material in the crock, and with your hands, thoroughly and gently mix all the ingredients together. Cover and leave in the crock for at least one month.

Containers for the finished pot-pourri may be small bowls with lids, or old-fashioned open bowls with no lids, or containers with small holes in them for the perfume to escape. This mixture can also go into 'sweet bags' or, without the orris powder, spices and essential oils, into sleep pillows. The perfume mellows with time, becomes more fragrant, if a little fainter, with the years. A warm atmosphere will help draw the fragrance out; shaking the bowl, or stirring the mixture with the hand will also release the perfume. A few more dried flowers and leaves, and some extra drops of essential oil can be added to give new vitality to a faded mixture.

Lavender pot-pourri

1 cup English lavender flowers
½ cup marjoram leaves
1 tablespoon thyme leaves
1 tablespoon mint leaves
1 tablespoon orris root powder
2 teaspoons ground coriander
¼ teaspoon ground cloves
a few drops lavender oil

Mix the flowers and leaves together. Blend the orris powder, coriander and cloves separately, then stir in the lavender oil and add to the dried material. This mixture may go into sachets or into bowls.

Note: The quantities given are for dried flowers and foliage.

Crystallized flowers

The following method is the simplest and quickest way to crystallize flowers. Whole small blooms, or single petals may be used, the most suitable being violets, borage flowers, rosemary flowers, English primroses, rose petals and small, whole rosebuds. (The various scented mint leaves are excellent too.)

Put the white of an egg into a saucer, break it up with a fork, but do not whip. Take a dry flower, or a single petal, and with a small paint brush dipped into the egg white, cover it completely, then shake caster sugar through a fine sieve over the flower, first on one side, then the other. As they are finished, spread them out on greaseproof paper laid in a small oven dish. Put the flowers in a very slow oven with the door open for approximately 10-15 minutes, gently turning them as the sugar hardens. Do not leave too long or they will go brown. Store the candied flowers between layers of greaseproof paper in an airtight box.

Beauty face pack

Natural face packs and lotions work magically on the skin, giving a dewy glow and lovely texture. Fennel seed helps smooth lines away; chamomile is astringent and anti-inflammatory; sage is cooling and astringent; elder flowers lighten and soothe the skin and are especially good for helping to fade freckles. Yoghurt and honey feed, clear and stimulate the skin. Fuller's earth contains minerals. For dilated veins on the face, do not use a face pack or extremes of heat and cold. Bathe with tepid milk, leaving it to dry on the face before gently washing off with lukewarm water.

1 cup water
2 teaspoons of any of the following herbs:
fennel seeds
chamomile flowers
sage leaves
elder flowers
100 g (3½ oz) plain yoghurt
1 tablespoon honey
1 tablespoon Fuller's earth (available from chemist)

Simmer herbs in water for 15 minutes. Strain into a small bowl (makes about 1 tablespoon strong liquid). Add yoghurt, honey and Fuller's earth. Mix well together. Cool in the refrigerator. Cleanse face thoroughly. Apply pack lightly with cotton wool, all over the face and neck. Lie down for 15 minutes. To remove pack, rinse well with cotton wool, repeatedly dipped into warm water or a strained herb tea of your choice. Pat dry.

Anti-freckles cream

28 ml (1 fl oz) lemon juice
¼ teaspoon powdered borax
3.5 ml (½ drachm) oil of rosemary

Mix well and let stand for a few days before using. Rubbed on the hands and face, cream will lighten, and finally disperse freckles.

Anti-freckles lotion

56.5 g (2 oz) tincture of benzoin
3.5 ml (½ drachm) oil of rosemary
28 g (1 oz) tincture of talc

Mix the ingredients well together in a corked bottle. When required for use, add a teaspoon of the mixture to a wineglass of water and apply the lotion where required night and morning, gently dabbing it in with a soft cloth.

Hand lotion

5 parts glycerine
15 parts rosewater

Mix well together. Soft water, elderflower or other herb water can be used instead of rosewater. When using herb water, add a pinch of borax.

Balm tea for strengthening the memory

28 g (1 oz) balm
568 ml (1 pint) boiling water

Infuse the balm in the water for 15 minutes. Allow to cool. Drink freely. Sugar and lemon juice give this infusion a pleasant taste.

To whiten the teeth

Rub with sage leaves.

Wash for the hair

112 ml (4 fl oz) lavender water
14 g (½ oz) borax
84 ml (3 oz) rosewater
7 g (¼ oz) tincture of cochineal

After washing the hair in this solution, rinse well, with a little borax in the last water. This wash is particularly good for oily hair.

Tonic and restorative for the hair   1

Infuse in vinegar: rosemary, sage, southernwood. Allow to stand in bottle in a sunny window for seven or eight days before straining.

Tonic and restorative for the hair   2

Infuse in olive oil: sage, thyme, marjoram and balm (all "live-for-ever" herbs). Prepare as for above recipe. Rub a little into scalp before shampooing.

Sage hair tonic

1 tablespoonful each of tea and of dried sage

Put into 1 kg (2 lb) jam jar, cover with boiling water, and simmer for two hours. Cool and strain. Rub into scalp four or five times a week. Gradually greyness will disappear, and hair will become dark brown. Tonic will keep for a week. Add 1 tablespoonful of rum, gin, or Eau-de-Cologne for longer keeping.

Bronchitis and tightness of the chest

Chop a garlic small and put into a jar of vaseline. Stand on a warm hob for a few days. When cold, massage freely into back and chest.

To cure corns

Take equal parts of a roasted onion and soft soap. Beat well together and apply them to the corn on linen, as a poultice.

To relieve a heavy cold

Grate horseradish and inhale the fumes that arise.

Anti-moth herbs   1

A handful each of dried and crumbled santolina, wormwood, mint, tansy; half a stick of cinnamon cut up small. A few dried pyrethrum flowers.

Anti-moth herbs   2

A handful each of lavender, rosemary, southernwood, thyme. A little penny-royal, 14 g (½ oz) crushed cloves, small piece of dried lemon peel.

Garlic garden spray

We have tried the following garlic spray against aphids, snails, cabbage moth, caterpillars and mosquitoes, with considerable success, especially when carried out at 2 weekly intervals.

85 g (3 oz) (about 3 big knobs) garlic, unpeeled
6 tablespoons medicinal paraffin oil
1 tablespoon oil-based soap, grated
0.5 L (1 pint) hot water

Roughly chop garlic, put into blender with paraffin oil and pulverise. Scrape resulting pulp into a bowl, cover and leave for 48 hours. Stir grated soap into hot water until melted. Stir soap and water into garlic mixture. When cool, strain into screw-top jars and store in refrigerator. For spraying in the garden, use 2 tablespoons of garlic solution to 2L (4 pints) water.

HERB CHART

HERB	SOUPS	SNACKS & SAVOURIES
BASIL	Tomato, pea or potato soup	Herb sandwiches, dips, tomato savouries
BAY LEAVES	All soup and stock	Flavours paté, terrines
BOUQUET GARNI	All soups	Bechamel sauce
CARAWAY SEED	Potato soup	Cream cheese dips and spreads
CHIVES	Chilled soups, vichysoisse	Herb sandwiches, dips, spreads, garnish
CINNAMON	Sprinkle on fruit soups	Cinnamon toast, waffles; bark used to stir black coffee
CORIANDER	Curry Soup	Ground in pickles
CUMIN	Curry Soup	Ground in pickles
DILL (leaves and seed)	Leaves as soup garnish	Leaves in garlic bread, herb sandwiches; leaves an seed in sauce and dips
GARLIC FLAKES POWDER	All soups	Garlic bread; powder in sauces, dips
MARJORAM	Beef stock	Herb sandwiches, marjoram vinegar
MINT	Garnish on soup	Herb sandwiches
OREGANO	Tomato, pea soup	Pizza, in olive marinade, cheese savouries, herb bread
PARSLEY	Vegetable, tomato fish soups; as garnish	Herb sandwiches, in dips, herb bread; garnish on hot-savouries
ROSEMARY	Beef and mutton stock	Herb bread and scones, dumplings; liver paté
SAGE	Minestrone, chicken soup	Meatballs, cheese savouries, herb bread, Welsh rarebit
TARRAGON	Fish soup	Tarragon vinegar, sauce tartare, chicken, livers, paté
THYME	Beef broth, vegetable soup, chicken soup	Meat balls, cheese savouries, paté

EGGS, BEEF, POULTRY, FISH	VEGETABLES & SALAD	SWEET
Meat loaf, veal, spaghetti bolognaise, salmon or tuna	Salads, over tomatoes, in mashed potato, eggplant, marrow	
Steamed fish, oxtail stew, all casseroles	Vegetable casseroles, lentil stew	A leaf on baked rice pudding, baked custard
All stews and casseroles	Vegetarian casseroles	
	Coleslaw, cooked carrots, cabbage, onion	Stewed fruit, seedcake bread
Egg dishes, barbecued meat, cold chicken	In salads, Idaho potatoes, mashed potatoes	
	A little sprinkled over glazed carrots, creamed spinach, baked sweet potato	Fruit pies, custard, cakes, biscuits
Ground in seasoning for veal, fish dishes, curries, oriental dishes	In oriental cooking	Fruit puddings, apple crumble, tea cake
Ground in seasoning, for veal, fish dishes, curries, oriental dishes	Ground in oriental cooking	Fruit puddings, apple crumble, tea cake
Leaves in fish, shellfish, egg and cheese dishes	Seeds in coleslaw, salad; leaves in vegetable stew, buttered vegetables	Seed in cakes and bread; seed tea aids digestion
Steak Diane, grills, stews, casseroles	Salads and French Dressing	
Meat loaf, veal, steak	Potatoes, vegetable casseroles	Herb scones
In egg dishes, mint sauce with lamb	With buttered peas, mashed potato	Mint ice, mint julep
Spaghetti bolognaise, Italian dishes, veal, egg dishes	In salads, potato salad; with cooked potato, artichokes, tomatoes	
Egg dishes, hamburgers, stuffings for meat and poultry; in tuna loaf	On Idaho potatoes, salad dressing, with potatoes, cauliflower, carrots	
With baked lamb, lamb casseroles, stews, chicken	Herb dressing, with eggplant, tomatoes, cabbage	
Meat loaf, chicken stuffing casseroles, omelettes	Leek tart, vegetarian stews	
Seafoods, chicken, egg dishes	In green salads	
Meat loaf, braised rabbit, chicken, stuffing, egg dishes, liver	Tomatoes, broccoli, beans, lentil stew	

HERB TEA CHART

A HERBAL TEA FOR 1 PERSON IS MADE BY POURING 1 CUP OF BOILING WATER INTO 1 TEASPOON OF HERBS, COVER, LET STAND FOR A FEW MOMENTS, THEN STRAIN. INCREASE THE NUMBER OF TEASPOONS AND BOILING WATER FOR EACH EXTRA PERSON.

A herbal tea is an infusion of boiling water and herbs, either fresh or dried, and may be taken first thing in the morning, during the day, and before going to bed. Each herb tea has different benefits, and is often a remedy for a mild indisposition. Many people assert that taking these teas over a long period builds up a resistance to a number of illnesses. Most herbs teas are pleasant to drink. No milk is added. Honey, or a squeeze of lemon, or both if you wish, may be stirred into the tea. Two teas may be mixed together (especially if the flavours are complementary) thereby giving a two-fold benefit. A litre may be made at the beginning of the day and stored in the refrigerator. Peppermint tea, roschip tea, and lemongrass tea are especially pleasant when iced, and all are refreshing to drink in the summer. Ice cubes and long stalks of fresh, leafy herbs and a dash of fruit juice or mineral water, all help to enhance the taste of cold herb teas in hot weather.

HERB	NERVE SEDATIVE	DIGESTION	RHEUMATIC PAIN	COUGHS & COLDS	POOR SKIN	GENERAL/ BLOOD TONIC	HEART TONIC	KIDNEY TONIC	LIVER TONIC
Angelica	★	★		★	★	★			
Anise		★		★	★				
Balm	★	★		★	★		★	★	
Basil			★	★	★		★	★	
Bay	★	★	★	★	★				
Borage	★		★		★	★	★	★	
Caraway		★			★			★	
Chamomile	★	★		★	★				★
Chervil			★		★	★		★	★
Chicory		★			★				★
Chives		★				★		★	★
Comfrey		★		★	★	★			
Coriander		★			★	★			
Cress	★				★	★			
Dill	★	★		★		★			★
Fennel		★			★				
Garlic	★	★	★	★	★	★		•	
Horseradish		★		★	★	★			
Lavender	★	★	★		★				
Lovage		★		★	★	★		★	
Marjoram & Oregano	★	★	★	★		★			
Parsley			★		★	★		★	
Peppermint	★	★		★		★			★
Rosemary	★	★					★	★	
Sage	★	★				★			★
Salad Burnet	★		★		★	★			
Savory		★			★	★			
Spearmint		★		★					★
Tarragon		★				★			
Thyme	★	★		★	★	★		★	

Reference books

Armanino Farms, *Winter News Sheet*, San Francisco.

Coates, Peter, *Roses* (Weidenfeld and Nicolson, London, 1962).

Culpeper, Nicholas, *Culpeper's Complete Herbal* (W. Foulsham and Co Ltd, London).

David, Elizabeth, *Spices, Salt and Aromatics in the English Kitchen* (Penguin Books, Harmondsworth, 1970).

Deans, Esther, *Esther Deans' Gardening Book* (Harper and Row (Australia) Pty Ltd, 1977).

Geuter, Maria, *Herbs in Nutrition* (Bio-Dynamic Agricultural Association, London, 1962).

Grieve, Mrs. M., *A Modern Herbal* 2 vols. Edited by Mrs. C.F. Leyel (Hafner Publishing Co, New York, 1959).

Hall, Dorothy, *The Book of Herbs* (Angus and Robertson Pty Ltd, Sydney, 1972).

Harmsworth's Universal Encyclopedia (Educational Book Co Ltd, London).

Hemphill, Rosemary, *Herbs and Spices* (Penguin Books, Harmondsworth, 1966).

Hemphill, Rosemary, *Herbs for All Seasons* (Angus and Robertson Pty Ltd, Sydney, 1972).

Horrocks, Lorna, *Natural Beauty,* (Angus and Robertson, 1980).

Janes, E.R., *Growing Vegetables for Show* (Penguin Books, Harmondsworth, 1956).

Leyel, Mrs. C.F., and Harley, Olga, *The Gentle Art of Cookery* (Chatto and Windus, London, 1925).

Little, Kitty, *Kitty Little's Book of Herbal Beauty* (Penguin Books, 1981).

Loewenfeld, Claire, *Herb Gardening* (Garden Book Club, London, 1964).

Lotions and Potions (Compiled by the National Federation of Women's Institutes, England, 1956, printed by Novello and Co Ltd).

Philbrick, Helen and Greeg, Richard B., *Companion Plants* (Stuart and Watkins, London 1967).

Ranson, Florence, *British Herbs* (Penguin Books, Harmondsworth, 1949).

Rohde, Eleanour Sinclair, *A Garden of Herbs* (Medici Society, London).

Rohde, Eleanour Sinclair, *The Old English Herbals* (Longman, Green and Co, London, 1922).

Rohde, Eleanour Sinclair, *Shakespeare's Wild Flowers* (Medici Society, London, 1963).

Sunset Books, *How to Grow Herbs* (Lane Books, Menlo Park, California, 1972).

Webster, Helen Noyes, *Herbs* (Charles T. Branfor Co, Boston, 1947).

Wilmot, Claire, *Triad Health Products,* Literature from St. Ives, N.S.W.

INDEX

A

Aioli 55, 106
Allantoin 44
Allium sativum 54-5
  schoenoprasum 42-3
  tuberosum 42-3
American upland cress 48
  wild mint 67
Anethole 21
Anethum graveolens 50-1
Angelica 18-9, 62
Angelica archangelica 18-9
Anise 20-1, 47
  star 21
Anthemis nobilis 35-7
Anthricus cerefolium 38-9
Anti-freckles cream 116
  lotion 116
  moth herbs 118
Ants 72
Aphids 55
Aphis 72
Applemint 67, 71
  golden 67
  variegated 67
Archemorous 73
Artemis dracunculus 87-9

B

Bacon Sir Francis 32
Baked broccoli with dill
  seed and sour cream 100
Balm 22-3, 66
  bee 29
  lemon, variegated 67
  tea 116
  variegated lemon 67
Basil 24-6, 32
  bush 24-6
  mint 67
  salmon and, loaf 110
  sweet 24-6
Bay laurel 27
  sweet 27

tree 27-8, 106, 111
Beauty face pack 115
Bee balm 29
Beetles, black flea 72
Beetroot in caraway
  port jelly 98
Belgian endive 40
Bergamot 29-30
  Cambridge Scarlet 29
  loaf, tomato and 105
  mint 67
  orange 29
Black flea beetles 72
Borage 26, 31-2, 45
Bouquet garni 28, 75, 92
Broccoli, baked with dill
  seed and sour cream 100
Bronchitis and tightness
  of the chest 118
Brown bread herb
  sandwiches 103
Bush basil 24-6

C

Cabbage root fly 93
Cambridge Scarlet
  bergamot 29, 30
Caraway 33-4, 38, 51, 98
Carrot fly 78
Carum carvi 33-4
Cat thyme 91
Caterpillars 85
  cabbage butterfly 72
Chamomile
  English 35-7, 115
  German 35-7
  Roman 35-7
  Treneague 35-7
Charlemagne, Emperor 75
Chaucer, Geoffrey 54, 70
Cherry laurel 27
Chervil 38-9, 43
Chicken and parsley
  pie 107
  salad 102

Chicory 40-1
  casserole 105
Chinese chives 42
  parsley 46
Chive butter 43
Chives 39, 42-3, 102, 103
  Chinese 42
  Garlic 42-3
  Onion 42-3
Cichorum intybus 40-1
Citrus bergamia 29
Cochlearis armoracia 56-7
Cold, to relieve 118
Comfrey 44-5
  fritters 101
  prickly 44
Companion plants 13
Complete Herbal 39, 42
Coriander 21, 46-7,
  53, 111
Cornmint 67
Corns, to cure 118
Corsican mint 67
Cress 48-9
  American upland 48
  curled 48
  French 48
  land 48-9
  water 48-9
Crinkly-leaved
  spearmint 69, 71
Crystallized flowers 114
Culpeper, Dr Nicholas
  34, 39, 42, 49, 52, 86
Cultivation 13
Curled cress 48
  parsley 73-5
Curried egg mousse 103
Cuttings 10-1

D

Deans, Esther 45
Derris Dust 13, 42
Dill 50-1, 103
Downy 43

E

Eau-de-Cologne mint
  67, 71, 103
Egyptian mint 67
Endive, Belgian 40
English chamomile 35-7
  sorrel 85
  spearmint 70
*Esther Deans' Gardening
  Book* 45
European horse mint 67
Evelyn, John 85

F

Face pack, beauty 115
Febrifuge 35
Fennel 34, 47, 50, 51, 115
  bulbs with cheese
    sauce 104
  Florence 52-3
Feverfew 35
Fines herbes 39, 43, 74, 93
Florence fennel 52-3
*Foeniculum vulgare
  dulce* 52-3
French beans and
  savory 101
  cress 48
  sorrel 85-86
  tarragon 87-9
Fritters, comfrey 101

G

Garden, herb layout 15
  spray, garlic 119
  thyme 106
*Gardening Book, Esther
  Deans'* 45
Garlic 28, 54-5, 106, 118
  bread 105
  garden spray 119
Gerard, John 44, 65
German chamomile 35-7
Ginger mint 67
Golden applemint 67
Graeps, spiced whole 111
Green cress soup 97
Gregg, Richard B. 13
Grey woolly thyme 91

H

Hair, tonic and
  restorative for 117
  wash for 117
Hamburg parsley 73
Hand lotion 116
Healthy brown rice and
  mint salad 100
Herb chart 120
  garden layout 15
  pillow 19, 23, 28, 37, 58,
    61, 66, 72
  sandwiches 103
  tea chart 123
Herbed leg of lamb 109
Homer 54
Horace 54
Horseradish 56-7, 118
  sauce 98
Hyll, Thomas 22

I

Illicium anisatum 21
Italian parsley 73-5

K

Knotted marjoram 65

L

Lamb, herbed leg of 109
Land cress 48-51
Laurel, bay 27
  cherry 27
  noble 27
  Roman 27
  true 27
Laurus nobilis 27-8
Lavanduala allardi 59
  dentata 58-61
  officinalis 58-61
  spica 58-61
  stoechas 58-61
Lavender 58-61
  English 58-61
  pot-pourri 114
  French 58-61
  Italian (or Spanish) 58-61
  sachets 113
  Spanish (or Italian) 58-61
Layout, herb garden 15
Lemon balm 22-3
  variegated 67
  mint 67
  thyme 90-3
Lepidium sativatum 48-9
Levisicum officinale 62-3
Liquorice mint 67
Lovage 62-3

M

Macaroni with sour cream
  and oregano 109
Marjoram 22, 23,
  64-6, 103
  butter 66
  knotted 65
  salmon and, pie 108
Matricaria chamomile 35-7
*Medical papyrus
  of Thebes* 47
Melissa officinalis 22
Mentha 67-72
  crispa 67, 69, 70-2
  piperita citrata 67, 71
  officinalis 67, 69, 70-72
  pulegium 67, 69, 72
  rotundiflora 67, 71
  spicata 67, 69, 70-2
  viridis 67, 69, 70-2
*Midsummer Night's
  Dream, A* 91
Mint 22, 29, 67-72
  American upland,
    wild 67
  apple 67, 71
  golden 67
  variegated 67
  basil 67
  bergamot 67
  Corsican
  eau-de-Cologne 67, 71
  Egyptian 67
  English spearmint 70
  European horse 67
  cornmint 67
  ginger 67
  golden apple 67
  lemon 67
  liquorice 67

orange 67
pennyroyal 67, 69-72
peppermint 67, 69, 70-2
pineapple 67
salad, healthy brown
  rice and 100
smooth-leaved
  spearmint 69
spearmint, 67, 69, 70-2
  crinkly-leaved 69, 71
  English 70
  smooth-leaved 69
variegated apple 67
Vietnamese 67
water 67
woolly 67
Minted honey soufflé 111
Mixed herbs 80, 92
Monarda didyma 29-30
Monardez, Nicholas 29
Mountain sorrel 85
Moutarde des
  Allemands 56
mucilage 45
mustard

N

Nasturtium officinale 48-9
Noble laurel 27

O

Ocimum basilicum 24-6
  minimum 24-6
Onion chives 42-3
Orange mint 67
Oregano 22, 28, 64-6, 86
  butter 66
  macaroni with sour
    cream and 109
Origanum majorana 64-6
  vulgare 64-6
Oswego tea 29
Oxtail and lentil stew,
  thick 106

P

Parsley 28, 39, 43, 73-5,
  99, 103, 106
  butter 74

chicken and, pie 107
Chinese 46
Hamburg 73
Italian 73-5
Pawpaw seed dressing
  with parsley 99
Pectin 19
Pennyroyal 14, 67, 69-72
Peppermint 37, 67,
  69, 70-2
Pepys' Diary 79
Pestou 25, 26, 99
Petroselinum crispum 73-5
  neopolitanum 73-5
Philbrick, Helen 13
Pimpinella anisum 20-1
Pineapple mint 67
Pliny 40, 52, 54
Pot-pourri 19, 23, 28, 30,
  58, 61, 66, 72, 78, 113
  lavender 114
Powdery mildew 43
Prickly comfrey 44
Propagating herbs 10-2
Prostrate rosemary 76-8
Prunus laurocerasus 27

R

Recipes 94-119
Roast tarragon
  chicken 107
Roman chamomile 35
Roman laurel 27
Rosemary 14, 22, 28,
  76-8, 100, 116
  butter 77
  prostrate 76-8
  upright 76-8
  zucchini 100
Rosmarinus officinalis 76-8
  prostratus 76
Rumex scutatus 85-6
Russian tarragon 87

S

St. Mark 59
Sage 22, 78-80, 102, 103,
  115, 116
  hair tonic 117
  Welsh rarebit 102

Salad burnet 81-2, 103
  chicken 102
Salmon and basil loaf 110
  marjoram pie 108
Salvia officinalis 79-80
Sandwiches, brown
  bread herb 103
Sanguisorba minor 81-2
Satureia hortensis 83-4
  montana 83-4
  repondeus 83
Savory 83-4
  butter 84
  French beans and 101
  summer 83-4
  winter 83-4
Scab 43
Seeds 12
Shakespeare, William
  54, 59, 70, 83, 91
Sheep's sorrel 85
Silver Posie thyme 90-1
Smallage 62
Smooth-leaved
  spearmint 69
Sorrel 97
  English 85
  French 85-6
  mountain 85
  sheep's 85
  soup 97
Soup, green cress 97
  sorrel 97
Spearmint 67, 69,
  70-2, 111
  butter 71
  crinkly-leaved 69, 71
  English 70
  smooth-leaved 69
Spiced whole grapes 111
Star anise 21
Summer savory 83-4
Sweet basil 24-5
  bay 27
Symphytum officinale 44-5

T

Tagetes minuta 87
Tarragon 39, 43, 103
  butter 89
  chicken, roast 107

French 87-9
Russian 87
winter 87
Tea chart, herb 123
Thick oxtail and lentil
  stew 106
Thyme 22, 28, 61, 90-3
  cat 91
  garden 90-3, 106
  grey woolly 91
  lemon 90-3
  Silver Posie 90, 91
  variegated lemon 90
  Westmoreland 90, 91
Thymus vulgaris 90-3
Tomato and bergamot
  loaf 105
Tonic and restorative for
  the hair 117

Treneague chamomile 35
True laurel 27

U

Upright rosemary 76-8
Urtica dioica 19

V

Variegated applemint 67
  lemon balm 67
  thyme 90
Vietnamese mint 67
Virgil 54, 83

W

Wash for the hair 116

Water cress 48-51
Watermint 67
Weevils 55
Welsh rarebit, sage 102
Westmoreland thyme 90-1
Whiten teeth, to 116
White wax scale 27
Wilmot, Clare 99
Woolly mint 67
Winter savory 83-4
  tarragon 87
Winter's Tale, The 59, 83
Witloof 40

Z

Zucchini, Rosemary 100

Blandford Press

an imprint of
Cassell Publishers Limited
Villiers House, 41/47 Strand
London WC2N 5JE

© Copyright: John and Rosemary Hemphill 1983
© Copyright design: Kevin Weldon & Associates Pty Limited

First published by Lansdowne Press, Sydney 1983
First published in Great Britain 1984
Reprinted 1984, 1985, 1986, 1987, 1988, 1989, 1990 ,1991, 1992 , 1993 ,1994

ISBN 0 7137 1451 4

Distributed in the United States by
Sterling Publishing Co., Inc.,
387 Park Avenue South, New York, NY 10016–8810

Designed by Mark Newman
Typeset in Australia in Bembo Roman 9pt by
Deblaere Typesetting Pty Ltd
Printed in Singapore by
Kyodo Printing Co (S'pore) Pte Ltd